D0380727

HAMMERED BY THE IRISH

How the Pitstop Ploughshares disabled a U.S. war-plane —with Ireland's blessing

HARRY BROWNE

HAMMERED BY THE IRISH

How the
Pitstop Ploughshares
disabled a U.S. war-plane
—with Ireland's blessing

HARRY BROWNE

Introduction by Daniel Berrigan

CounterPunch
PETROLIA

PRESS

First published by
CounterPunch and AK Press 2008
© *CounterPunch* 2008
All rights reserved

CounterPunch
PO Box 228 Petrolia, California, 95558

AK Press
674A 23rd St, Oakland, California 94612-1163

ISBN 978-1904859901

A catalog record for this book is available from the Library of Congress

Library of Congress Control Number: 2008929304

Typeset in Minion Pro, designed by Robert Slimbach for Adobe Systems Inc.; and Futura, originally designed by Paul Renner. Cover and Title Page use Neutraface Condensed Titling and Neutraface Text, designed by Christian Schwartz for House Industries.

Printed and bound in Canada.

Index by Jeffrey St. Clair.
Cover Design by Tiffany Wardle.
Design and typography by Tiffany Wardle.

Contents

To Deirdre, Nuin, Karen, Damien and Ciaron

From: Naval Air Systems Command (PMA207)
Subj: US NAVY C-40A AIRCRAFT 165833 REPAIR ESTIMATES

1. The repair estimates provided by Boeing Aircraft Company to Naval Air Systems Command, C-40A Program Management staff...

Nose Radome	New
Engine Spinner	New
Fan Cowl	Leased/Repaired
Exhaust Plugs	Leased/Repaired
Fuselage Skins	New
T/R Cowl	Leased/Repaired
Nose Strut	New
Repairs	
Hardware	
Boeing AOG Team	
Transportation costs	
Lease costs	

Total: **$2,715,000.00**

Acknowledgments

I am indebted to the Pitstop Ploughshares and others for the memories and documents they made available to me.

Among the documents was Ciaron O'Reilly's pre-publication copy of Sharon Erickson Nepstad's important *Religion and War Resistance in the Plowshares Movement* (New York: Cambridge University Press).

The Irish Republic, the United States and the Iraq War: A Critical Appraisal is an extremely valuable study by Dr Kieran Allen and Dr Colin Coulter, prepared for the Irish Anti-War Movement in 2003 and liberally harvested here. It remains available online through irishanti-war.org.

The extraordinary archives of Indymedia Ireland (indymedia.ie) provided a great deal of telling, gap-filling and memory-jarring detail. Aoife Ní Dhalaigh's trial notes from July 2006, commissioned by Action from Ireland (AfrI), were also useful.

Thanks to Brendan Barrington of *Dublin Review* for commissioning a long article on the case and thus helping to make a longer book seem possible. Thanks to Catherine Cullen for such loving proofreading. And thanks of course to *CounterPunch* for allowing me over several years to spread the good news, and even occasionally the bad news, about war resistance in Ireland and the Pitstop Ploughshares.

Introduction

There are two aspects of Harry Browne's *Hammered by the Irish* that I really am grateful for.

The first is competence, something I could take for granted with this writer, and which allows an important story to unfold with clarity.

The second is that the author takes sides. He avoids any of the journalistic shibboleths of 'objective reporting'. In fact, while the events about which he writes were ongoing, he made himself part of the support activity around the case and the trials, something that must have been wonderfully heartening for the young defendants who found themselves so endangered by the system. Browne was and is visibly on their side.

This book, like its author, is not guilty of being a mere bystander. It is prepared to be passionate about issues of life and death, the central issues that the Pitstop Ploughshares case was really about, though the court could not begin to acknowledge that fact until it was finally given over to a jury of ordinary decent people.

The courts too often become part of a vast network of injustice. That was true in the case of the Pitstop Ploughshares until their third trial was well under way. We in the United States are accustomed to a 'justice' system that colludes with injustice: in time of war, particularly, everything is sucked into a vortex of violence and complicity, so there is no chance of justice at all. It was shocking and disappointing to see that this process was at work in Ireland as well.

Browne finds much to praise in the eloquence and truth-telling of the five people who took this action at Shannon Airport. They were in many ways ideal defendants, well versed in the tradition of non-violence and upholding it in court, as elsewhere. They were forceful when necessary, without being overbearing.

Personally, I am proud that these five people and this action upheld and honored a specific tradition that we started in 1980 and that has since resulted in Plowshares actions all over the world. They have stood for non-violence, and for the idea that certain weapons, and wars such as the one against the people of Iraq, should have no place in the world.

— Daniel Berrigan
New York City, June 5, 2008

Prologue

TUESDAY, JULY 25th 2006, DUBLIN: THERE HAVE BEEN TIMES when I've attended this court like a proper journalist, more or less, but today isn't one of them. The third trial of the people known to the media as the Shannon Five, and to supporters as the Pitstop Ploughshares, has reached the jury-deliberation stage, and a verdict could come at any time. But since my partner Catherine is doing a day's paid work and I'm not, it's up to me to look after Stella, our 16-month-old. I take her down to the Liffey-side quay and Dublin's majestic "Four Courts" complex, but after a brief attempt to keep her quiet in the courtroom while Judge Miriam Reynolds explains that she is not going to accede to the jury's request that they see the actual legislation under which the Five are charged, Stella and I take our rightful place at the 'vigil' under a little tree at the corner of the courthouse.

Here, through three trials in the last year-and-a-half, under the gaze of sporadic pedestrian traffic and the city's constant vehicular crawl, the defendants and their supporters have set up a makeshift shrine of photos and names for the Iraq war dead, along with a banner or two. On one of them you can see where the words "War on Trial" have been sewn over with a patch inscribed "Peace on Trial". This happened after the prosecuting lawyer, in the first trial, accused the defendants of trying to hijack solemn legal proceedings for inappropriate purposes, i.e. to put the US-led war in the dock. In other times and places such defendants might have replied, "Yeah, so?" Not these defendants, though. They have carefully placed their case in the hands of a rigorously professional legal team, and that has meant making a few adjustments – even to the propaganda with which they address the world outside the court (their website name underwent the same metamorphosis).

During court sessions, the vigil here is thinly populated – all the more so today, with excitement stirring indoors. The indefatigable Colm Roddy, out of his orange 'Guantánamo' jumpsuit in this warm weather, wears a sign denouncing the use of Shannon Airport in the US war and occupation; Marta, a Japanese Buddhist monk who normally resides in the English city of Milton Keynes, keeps up the rhythm on a little prayer drum; independent video-maker Eamonn Crudden assembles his equipment in anticipation of getting the crucial post-verdict footage outdoors – hopeful that the defendants will actually be leaving the courthouse on foot today rather than in a prison van. There is room for Stella to run around – only a bit of broken glass for her to avoid, perhaps from disgruntled folks flinging bottles at the courthouse – and as on the previous occasions when we've set down here, she makes a picturesque addition to the peaceful, peace-loving scene. Or so I think, though I'm sure many passers-by are adding 'child abuse' to their mental list of the anti-war movement's sins.

William Hederman comes over for a chat. A tall, good-looking, still-young guy who has shrugged off his family's wealth and political connections, along with a promising career at the *Irish Times*, he is now very much an independent, 'movement' journalist, and the only established professional hack other than myself who has been in frequent and careful attendance at this case. (A couple of young court-reporters have flitted in and out, but with these trials often tied up in legal argument, the copy has been getting pretty thin.) The buzz, he says, is good. Indeed, it has been good ever since Judge Reynolds ruled last Wednesday that the defence could make their case that the five had a statutory 'lawful excuse' to attack a US Navy aircraft with the intention of saving lives by doing so. The judge has read and explained the relevant passage of the statute to the jury in great detail; now watchers seem to reckon that the jury's desire to see it for themselves means they think the case's facts justify the defence argument, but some of them may just want "to be sure to be sure" (to misuse that Irishism) before signing off on an acquittal. I think that seems an unjustifiably optimistic reading of events, but then I was away yesterday and had to carry Stella out of court this morning before the jury came in for further clarification, so my own more cautious reading is second-hand and lacks the benefit of nuance and body-language.

A rumour runs down the riverside that the jury is returning, but by the time we've passed through the metal detectors and into the busy courtyard, it's clear the rumour was false. The defendants, lawyers and perhaps 20 or 30 other people, mostly familiar anti-war faces, are crowded on steps outside court 23, and in a little roadway below. Laughter is everywhere, cigarette smoke is only slightly less ubiquitous, there is palpable eagerness in the air, and all these people seem geared up for celebration. I wonder can I have really missed so much in the courtroom, or is there some secret Irish airborne vibration of acquittal, of vindication, that an American like me, living here just 20 years, couldn't hope to pick up Stella, born a mile or two from here just after the first mistrial was declared in March 2005, seems to get it, and is enjoying all the attention and excitement, the chatter and giddiness of the scene.

Suddenly: "the jury's coming back." They could just have another question or request for the judge, but everyone crowds quickly toward the door, whatever may be about to happen inside. The diminutive Scottish defendant, Karen Fallon, sweeps Stella into her arms to carry her inside. Superintendent John Kerins, a cop who has been prosecuting this case for three-and-a-half years, gives Karen an astonishingly warm grin and mouths that there is, in fact, a verdict. Inside, all the cops and court officials seem to be smiling. I take Stella from Karen and take a place in the back row: in this rather small courtroom that is only three wooden benches behind the defendants. Stella is on my lap. Defendant Damien Moran's Polish girlfriend Dorota is beside me, next to his Offaly parents.

Inevitably, familiarly, there are a few minutes of apparently pointless milling around as we wait for judge and jury to enter. Then a couple of the defence barristers lean across the assembled supporters and warn us quietly that we shouldn't give any audible reaction to the verdict. This is the first that most of us who didn't hear the policeman's whisper have heard that a verdict is imminent, after a total of only three hours or so of deliberation, and the eagerness ratchets up another notch.

Then suddenly it's happening. The judge is in place, the jury has handed some paper to the clerk, who has shown it to the judge, then taken it back to read aloud, count by count, to the jury's fore-woman for confirmation. Stella is hushed, like everyone else. There are 10 counts of criminal damage to get through, two for each accused, but we know the whole story from the very first count: Ciaron O'Reilly, the big dreadlocked Aussie who is the nearest this group gets to a ringleader, is declared "not guilty" on the first charge – breaking a hangar window, a lesser offence that a fussy jury might just have convicted on to make the point that damaging Irish airport property is wrong, even when hammering the might of the American military machine is justifiable. If Ciaron has got off on that one, it's a clean sweep. Fifty people exhale simultaneously. Stella claps, quietly.

What is an audible reaction? As the clerk repeats the legal formula, always with the same outcome ("Do you the jury find the defendant Deirdre Clancy not guilty of…") and the jury nods, I can hear sniffling and sobbing all around me; I feel I can almost hear the tension drain from the defendants' bodies as they slump toward each other in relief. I'm crying, quietly, and the thoughts behind my tears are probably no different from those of most of the people in the room: our friends, who were ready for prison and spent weeks inside on remand in 2003, won't have to go back; this jury of ordinary decent Dubliners saw the good in them and what they did; in February 2003 in Ireland, it was not a crime for them to go to County Clare, cut through a fence at 3am, crawl across a runway, break into a hangar and knock holes and lumps into an American military aircraft. And this is A Small Good Thing in the context of so much evil and suffering, of the terrible violence in Iraq, of

Israeli bombs raining on Lebanon, of the murderous criminals running the US and Britain and the complicitous ones running Ireland.

The judge tells the five they are free to go, then leaves the room herself. That gives us our chance to applaud the jury as they rise to leave, and we take it, cautiously first, then more robustly – drawing Judge Reynolds back in to chastise us and urge us out of her courtroom. Out we go, back-slapping all the way, leaving the defendants inside to get their heads together. Journalists arrive within minutes, and the Five's solicitor, Joe Noonan, has a press release ready for them, explaining the historic points of law that won the case. This scarcely sates the media, and by the time the five appear and exit through the gate there is a veritable crush of cameras, microphones and notebooks to press them back against the railings for soundbites. They deliver them ably, with Nuin Dunlop's American voice rising to especially poignant heights – even as she speaks, her embassy in Dublin is preparing a statement of "concern", expressing a desire to talk to the Irish government about the verdict that has vindicated this US citizen and her comrades.

To be honest, the jury's decision is a delight, and it has won the Shannon Five these 15 minutes of fame, but they didn't need it for vindication, not in my eyes. As an earnest American who has tried for 20 years to adjust to Irish people's typical cynicism and undemonstrative nature (at least while sober), I find an emotional and moral truth in these five people – two Irish-born and three of diaspora descent – that resonates almost unbearably, almost accusingly, and fills me with embarrassing love for them, each of them and all of them. In the 22 years after my father, an Irish-American New York Catholic priest, died in 1980, on the same day as Dorothy Day, I had long since become an atheist and stopped talking and thinking about Catholic Worker, a movement Father Harry Browne admired and drew upon for political sustenance. Father Phil Berrigan was arrested by duplicitous Feds in my dad's Upper West Side closet in 1970. And now Berrigan's name has been scrawled on an Irish airport, his moral descendents have found me in Dublin – and no one has ever seemed more self-evidently 'right' to me. A jury could have convicted them and a judge sent them down for 10 years and there would have been not a ripple on the calm certainty of my judgment, which comes from my deepest places.

I don't have any questions for them, I don't need to hear all the ones coming from the assembled press, and I do need to get my baby out of this crush, so I bring her back to the 'shrine' to run around and await our friends. They join us, the ex-defendants and a couple of dozen supporters; Stella gets passed around a bit and everyone holds a little circle-of-hands prayer ceremony, the Pitstop Ploughshares pouring splashes of bottled water and invoking the US and Iraqi dead. The red lights on the TV cameras start switching off at the sincere weirdness of it all.

At the edge of the crowd a juror explains: "Sometimes you just have to do the right thing."

Chapter 1

An Irish Solution

N AUGUST 2002, THE MOVEMENT TO OPPOSE A US-LED INVASION
of Iraq was beginning to take shape all around the world. And if you
were sitting in an astonishingly large public meeting in Dublin on
the 14th of that month, you could well believe that the Irish section of it
might include a strong and well-supported dimension of militant, albeit
non-violent, direct action.

The meeting, "War is Terror is War", had come together after 81-year-
old peace activist and Jesuit priest Daniel Berrigan said he was planning a vacation in Ireland, one in a long line of such visits over many
years, from his home in New York City. Berrigan and his Irish contacts
expected a small, intimate gathering. But as the date approached it
became clear that interest and excitement about his visit was a great deal
higher than anyone might reasonably have expected, and it swelled to a
fever after sympathetic interviews with him, conducted by telephone,
appeared in the weekend newspapers – including the all-important bible
of Dublin's better-off liberals, the *Irish Times*. A meeting that was initially expected to fit cosily in the corner of a pub, and had then been
scheduled for a function room in a city-centre hotel, was diverted by the
main organising group, Action from Ireland (AfrI), to one of the largest
venues in Dublin city centre, the cavernous O'Reilly Hall (named for
its benefactor, Irish media mogul Tony O'Reilly). This modern hall is
crammed into a corner of the Georgian complex at Belvedere College,
the still-posh Jesuit-run high school in the still-impoverished north

inner city, the home-territory of Leopold Bloom's fictitious rambles and James Joyce's real childhood.

Close to 1,000 people can be accommodated in the hall's steeply pitched seating, but even people who arrived early for the meeting's scheduled 8pm start – starting times usually being treated as a vague fiction in the world of Irish political gatherings – found an enormous queue stretching down Great Denmark Street. It was quickly clear that they would not all fit even in the O'Reilly Hall. Hundreds of them were shunted into another room, where they could hear an audio feed of the meeting. Hundreds more abandoned the queue and headed off to the pictures or the pub. Incredibly, it seemed that something approaching 2,000 people had turned up on a Tuesday night in what is usually the very quietest time of the year, when the city is abandoned to tourists, to hear the thoughts of an octogenarian legend of American peacemaking. No 21st century anti-war activity of any sort in Ireland up to that time could have expected to attract that kind of number.

The message that the gathered crowd heard from Berrigan was simple and could be summed up by the meeting's title: "War is Terror is War" reflected sensitivity about 9/11, then still a fresh wound, but also a rejection of the 'War on Terror' as a means of achieving justice. Berrigan warned of the military ambitions of the "arrogant and vengeful" Bush regime, and called on Ireland to respect its own tradition of military neutrality (born in the Second World War, when the country stayed out of an alliance with Britain, which had ceded limited independence to part of the island in 1922) by refusing to co-operate with and facilitate the American war-plans for the Middle East. There was little new in Berrigan's speech, but there was clearly excitement about hearing the words from his own lips, not least because he was bringing the message from New York City, scene of the crime. He spoke of some of the 9/11 relatives who had assembled as 'Families for Peaceful Tomorrows' (borrowing words from Martin Luther King) to oppose the wars being fought and prepared in the names of their loved ones.

In fact, much of the excitement of Berrigan's presentation was reliant on his 'real presence' in the room, because he spoke slowly and a little wanderingly, like the jet-lagged senior citizen he was. His fellow American at the table that sat at the front of the hall's proscenium stage, Father John Dear, was a good deal more dynamic. Dear was an energetic, earnest and articulate priest with a lot of jail-time for anti-war activities behind him and, he seemed to suggest, the potential for more to come. He had been working directly as a counsellor with the bereaved 9/11 families and could speak straight from the streets of lower Manhattan about the way grief had been hijacked for ends that neither they nor other ordinary Americans really wanted to support.

There was, it was obvious from the warm reception they got and the questions that followed their talks, overwhelming support for Berrigan and Dear. There was, however, another dynamic present in the room, as hundreds of progressive-minded Irish people sat listening to moral instruction from priests, perhaps scarcely believing they were doing so. By the turn of the millennium, many people were seriously talking about Ireland as a 'post-Catholic' country – without being sure at all what comes after Catholicism. The 1990s, in particular, had seen not only the predictable declines in religious piety and practice among a population that was getting rather quickly more wealthy and educated – in fact, the decline probably started first and most precipitously in some of the country's poorest communities – but also a succession of scandals that had decidedly knocked the Church off the pedestal it had occupied in the nation's public life.

Already, only 10 years on, people spoke nostalgically of the first of those big stories, the 1992 'Bishop Casey scandal'. "Ah, do you remember when the clerical sex scandal involved a consensual relationship with an adult woman?" The sensational story had seen the media-friendly and relatively left-leaning Bishop of Galway, Eamonn Casey, flee the country when the *Irish Times* revealed a 1970s love-affair with a young American, Annie Murphy – who had borne his child. Much more serious, everyone agreed, was the succession of horrible revelations that followed. Another camera-hungry member of the Irish Hierarchy, Bishop Brendan Comiskey of Ferns, was forced to resign in disgrace because of his cover-ups of some of the many, many, clerical abuse scandals that came to public attention in the 1990s.

While the media focussed on scandals, the disaffection of many liberal-minded Catholics had deeper roots. The conservative papal reign of John Paul II, who had halted any possible trend toward internal democracy and a loosening of strictures on personal sexuality, on clerical celibacy, on women priests, had further alienated many Catholics and ex-Catholics, in Ireland as elsewhere.

Of course, most of the Belvedere crowd that evening could make the distinction between that corrupt and hypocritical Church and the principled and courageous one represented by the men in front of them. Berrigan had, after all, made his feelings about the US Hierarchy clear, after the American bishops backed the invasion of Afghanistan: "Maybe," Berrigan said, "we should burn our copies of the gospels and process into our church sanctuaries holding aloft the Air Force Rule Book, with its command to kill our enemies, and incense that instead." Nonetheless, Ireland's Catholic-inflicted wounds still felt fresh, and were represented in the audience: one young man, in particular, kept questioning and then heckling the speakers on behalf of the victims of clerical abuse. Most of the audience didn't feel it would be appropriate to shout him down, but tensions began to rise as the torrent of complaints rained down on to the speakers. The meeting's chairperson, a superb and decidedly secular broadcaster, Roisin Boyd, seemed unsure how to handle the situation, which felt genuinely unprecedented. A burly, tattooed man rose from his seat near the back of the hall and started down the aisle toward the heckler, rolling up his sleeves, muttering that he was going to take care of this.

Then the third speaker from the platform intervened, verbally rather than physically. An Australian layman, well over six feet tall, dreadlocked and t-shirted, appearing younger than his 42 years, Ciaron O'Reilly (no relation to the hall) looked down from the stage with a fixed stare and told the heckler compassionately but commandingly that the institutional church which had let him down was the same one that had rejected the Berrigan tradition of peacemaking, that everyone shared and sympathized with his concerns and hurt but that tonight it was important to move on and talk about the coming war on Iraq and how to oppose it. The heckler went quiet, the tension abated and the burly would-be bouncer returned to his seat. O'Reilly's calm and calming intervention secured his status as the 'star' of this particular show.

He had already made a strong claim to this status with his riveting speech, full of passion and wisdom and self-deprecating humor about his part in anti-war actions in the US, Britain and his native Australia – and the prison spells in the first and last of those countries. And he was exciting the crowd with the imperative to act decisively and directly to oppose and prevent war and war preparations. Like the other two speakers, he spoke the language of the Catholic Worker tradition, founded in the 1930s in New York by Dorothy Day and Peter Maurin to give comfort to the poor and oppose war. Unlike the other two speakers, he was not a brief visitor but seemed inclined to stay in Ireland, if the banner behind him was to be believed: "Dublin Catholic Worker," it read. It had been made especially for this occasion, which was in some respects the group's coming-out party, four months after O'Reilly's arrival in the city.

It seemed extraordinary to think that in the nearly seven decades of the Catholic Worker's existence, there had never been a 'branch' – members would call it a community, or a house – in Ireland. Irish-Americans had long been involved in communities in the US – to the outsider it would appear the names Berrigan, Grady and Kelly loom largest in the movement's post-Day history – and houses had appeared to some small extent elsewhere in the world. O'Reilly, however, had become the first one to try to put down Catholic Worker roots in the Old Sod of Ireland.

It was in some respects a natural homecoming for O'Reilly, holder of an Irish passport. His immigrant ancestry did not lie in the distant mists of the Irish Famine of the 1840s but in the less romanticized, still-painful mass emigration of the 1950s, when his father left County Offaly, in Ireland's flat and boggy midlands, to settle in Brisbane, in Australia's Queensland. The most sharply reactionary part of an often profoundly conservative country, Queensland was run like a police state right through Ciaron's childhood and youth, with a police force that was heavily Irish-descended. Aboriginal people bore the brunt of the state's repressive apparatus, but rebellious young people could also expect to be forced into confrontation with the authorities.

That, certainly, was Ciaron's experience. From an early age his rebelliousness had a political dimension, with a commitment to peace and a sense of Australia's part in the war-making apparatus of the US nuclear-armed imperium. (In 1998, after more than two decades of thinking global, Ciaron acted local in a decisive manner, joining with comrades to 'disarm' uranium-mining equipment in his home country, then serving two stints in prison as a result.) In the late 1970s, still a teenager, he read about the Catholic Worker tradition. When, in 1980, Daniel and Philip Berrigan and six others entered a General Electric nuclear-warhead facility in King of Prussia, Pennsylvania, to hammer nosecones and introduce the modern activist tradition of 'Plowshares' (or in the Anglo-Irish-Australian spelling, Ploughshares), Ciaron O'Reilly was inspired. He founded a Catholic Worker community in Brisbane while attending college – he later qualified as a teacher, a job he pursued only occasionally in subsequent years – and started a life of virtually total devotion to working with the poor and waging peace.

The totality was neither accidental nor incidental. As Daniel Berrigan puts it, in the movement's most quoted quote: "Because we want peace with half a heart, half a life and will, the war making continues. Because the making of war is total – but the making of peace, by our cowardice, is partial."

It was a devotion whose trajectory would take Ciaron O'Reilly around the world. For a time O'Reilly lived at the centre of the empire, in Washington DC and New York – working with homeless people and living in Catholic Worker communities, befriending the Berrigans who had been his inspiration. He stayed at Jonah House in Baltimore, where Phil Berrigan and his partner Liz McAllister lived and worked and planned, the spiritual community centre of the young Plowshares tradition. Of the four years in total that Ciaron lived in the United States, about a year-and-a-half was spent as a guest of the Federal government – Dan Berrigan was fond of calling it a "Federal scholarship" – in US penitentiaries. This prison-sentence occurred as a result of his first Plowshares action, on New Year's Day 1991: along with a New Zealander and two Americans – they called themselves the Anzus Plowshares, based on the old wartime acronym for Australia, New Zealand and the US – he entered Griffiss Air Force base in upstate New York. While two of his comrades got to a B52 and used hammers to crack its fuselage, Ciaron and another colleague swung sledgehammers and knocked holes in the runway, forcing the halting of any flights taking place in the deployment to the Persian Gulf, where the US would unleash hell on Iraq just over two weeks later.

His prison stints took him even deeper into the American underclass than his work with homeless people – his white skin made him unusual in the US prison system, as in the Australian one – and made him all the more keenly aware of his privileges as an educated white man, strengthening his activist resolve. He was deported from the US after his sentence, and back home in Australia he concentrated on solidarity work with East Timor, challenging the complicity of his government in Indonesian repression.

The same concern for East Timor was at the centre of his activism when he moved to Britain in the mid-1990s. There he did trial-support work for the 'Seeds of Hope' Ploughshares. He did similar 'outside' work in Preston for the Swedish 'Bread Not Bombs' Ploughshares in 1998-99 and for the Jubilee Ploughshares in 2000-01.

The Seeds of Hope were especially significant. They were a group of women who damaged British Aerospace Hawk fighter-jets that were destined for Indonesia. Remarkably, especially for a veteran of the US Plowshares tradition like Ciaron O'Reilly, the Seeds of Hope women were acquitted of criminal damage in Liverpool in July 1996 by a majority jury verdict. The jury, by 10 votes to two, defied the trial judge's clear instruction that the defence justification for the action could not be deemed legitimate under the strict terms of the law. It was an enormous victory that indicated the potential of Ploughshares defendants to win over the 'conscience of the community' – as a jury is often called. It clearly indicated too that campaigners were winning the argument about East Timor, and it would be more difficult for Western governments to connive in its ongoing torture. East Timor's independence was to follow in 1999.

O'Reilly founded a Catholic Worker community in Liverpool, and later discovered that the group of peace activists he was involved in had been infiltrated by a spy – not from the notoriously spook-heavy British state but from British Aerospace, the weapons company that felt most threatened by campaigners' pressure. It was one of many aspects of his experience in Britain that alerted him to the complexities and difficulties of working in communities and on prolonged campaigns. His work with Andrea Needham of the Seeds of Hope group, and then with Angie Zelter, who started the Trident Ploughshares, also put him in a particularly strong position to observe how British activists had adapted Ploughshares activism in their own particular ways.

In one sense, once you get past the spelling there is no trans-Atlantic difference worth talking about. A Plowshares action is one in which activists determine to act directly against the machinery of war, doing damage that reflects the prophecies in the Old Testament books of Isaiah and Micah, in which it is suggested that swords will be beaten into plowshares, indicating that war will be obsolete. Or as Isaiah (2:4) is recorded as saying: "nations shall beat their swords into plowshares and their spears into pruning hooks; one nation shall not raise the sword against another, nor shall they train for war again." It's rich prophetic source material – not just the plowshares idea but the gospel cry "I ain't gonna study war no more" finds its origins there. Invariably, of course, the prophecy-turned injunction takes on particular cultural and personal inflections.

For one thing, and crucially, in Britain and elsewhere in Europe (notably, in the 1990s, Sweden) Ploughshares did not have the powerful, almost synonymous connection with the Catholic Worker that it did in the US. On America's east coast, where they were most common, Plowshares groups were often part of Catholic Worker communities. Those communities, among their many other activities, provided the basic infrastructure for Plowshares planning and support. Actions would be planned over months; potential 'actors' would go through a rigorous process of often-prayerful reflection and self-examination; they would be expected to have some more minor experience of arrest and jail before embarking on a path involving serious damage to Federal property and the felony conviction that was sure to follow.

American Plowshares activists, while much admired on the US Left, are on the fringe of a fringe of anti-war activity – i.e. they are a highly committed, hugely self-sacrificing and mostly religious element of the small direct-action section of the wider movement. Even relatively low-risk civil disobedience (blockades, occupations etc) has seemed less prominent in the early 21st century than it was in the anti-nuclear, Latin-American-solidarity, anti-apartheid and anti-sweatshop movements of the 1980s and '90s. Plowshares activity too peaked in the 1980s, when dozens of actions, many of them carried out by priests, nuns and other religious people, saw activists spend many years in American jails. (The median sentence was 18 months, but many were jailed for much, much longer.)

Drawing in part on the experience of Greenham Common, where women camped for years to oppose the presence of nuclear missiles in Britain, and probably influenced too by the highly publicized and anarchist-led environmental protests of the 1990s, the British tradition has evolved to become somewhat less secretive and insulated, rather more secular and Gandhian, than its US equivalent. For example, the Trident Ploughshares, named after the submarine-borne nuclear missiles they are dedicated to eradicating, are more or less permanently based near the Faslane Royal Navy base in Scotland. Rather than having 'members' who have been through the long rigors of preparation and then taken some particular action, the Trident group has 'pledgers' who are prepared to take action as required.

Perhaps equally significantly, the British Ploughshares in general also developed a more aggressive approach to legal strategy, setting out in court not merely to make a public point but to win cases by reference to international law and other useful instruments. In addition, US Plowshares campaigners keep careful count of the special actions that 'qualify' for the label, and name each of them according to some qualities of the 'target' or the people acting on it; the British for a time seemed ready to use the P-word wholesale.

In the end Britain's Trident Ploughshares movement developed its own taxonomy of actions, dividing them into 'minimum' and 'maximum disarmament' categories. The minimum category, inevitably a longer list, includes trespass actions that don't do direct damage to military equipment, and for which those arrested are unlikely to face significant jail time. (This distinction should not be seen as minimizing either the real potential risk to such activists or the potential political benefits of a sustained campaign of this sort of action.)

Despite the quasi-liturgical trappings of some Catholic Worker-based actions, in which prayer figures prominently and activists' blood often plays a part, neither the US nor the British traditions rely on any sectarian theological underpinning – the relevant prophetic quotes are from the Old Testament, holy to Christians and Jews, and there is also seen to be a clear basis for action in the provocative words and acts of Jesus himself. Nonetheless some campaigners look on the British tradition as a pragmatic, Protestant variant of Ploughshares, somewhat more middle-class in orientation, without the heavy Berriganesque emphasis on personal conscience and witness, and on the joys of jail. The British version takes actions and then expects to successfully justify them in court – the Americans, perhaps because they live in communities with a lot of contact with homeless people, tend to take a more jaded view of the law: they have been more likely to politicize their trials, get shouted at by the judge, and lose. These distinctions are of course simplistic: there is enormous cross-fertilisation, with, e.g., legal strategy becoming more important in the US movement. At any rate, it has become hard to generalize, when in fact full-fledged Plowshares actions (in the American sense) have been few and far between in recent years. Nonetheless the differences are real and Ireland's place between Britain and America is, as always, peculiar and complicated.

Ireland's traditional Catholicism did not make it particularly fertile ground for the Catholic Worker tradition of action, nor for its underlying philosophy of liberation theology. The term 'rebel priest' was reserved in Ireland for those understood to harbor particularly strong nationalist sentiments, and even a tolerance for the paramilitary expression of those sentiments in the form of the IRA. There were plenty of them. Prominent 'radical priests', on the contrary, you could probably count on one hand, and the best of them – e.g. Father Peter McVerry – were known for their tireless assistance to and outspoken advocacy for particular oppressed groups, such as homeless youth, not for their left-wing approach to foreign affairs. The odd missionary priest might get some publicity on that front.

Indeed, a millennium after the Irish Church had harboured some of the most extraordinary and even flamboyant artistic expressions of Western Christianity, the Irish approach to Catholicism had long become one that eschewed enthusiasm of all kinds. The 'well-liked priest' was often the man who combined superficial out-of-Church friendliness with a capacity to mutter his way through a quick and painless Sunday mass. The bit in the Catholic liturgy when the congregation is invited to exchange a sign of peace with fellow parishioners, used in much of the global Church as an opportunity for embraces, is treated in Ireland as an unwanted occasion to catch your neighbour's eye, murmur a greeting and share a barely-brushing handshake (you never know what you might catch). To an outsider, Irish Catholicism looks like it has entered some international competition to see which nation can best empty Christian rituals of any conceivable meaning, and it has won hands-down. (Its function as an expression of the Church's social power was the last meaning left to Irish Catholic practice, and that was more or less gone by the early 1990s.)

As for politics, it would be unfair to say the Irish Church has never expressed decent views on social justice and war. It is just that for many years those views were perceived as subordinate to its efforts to wield influence over people's sexuality and the state's role in regulating it. This had profound effects on how politics developed in the wider society: the late-20th-century 'Left' in Ireland, such as it was, arguably came to define itself less in terms of its commitment to economic equity and social justice than in opposition to the clerical pronouncements that dominated the State's positions on, e.g., contraception (liberalized only in the 1980s), divorce (introduced, with considerable restrictions, in the 1990s) and abortion (still illegal, with thousands of women traveling to Britain every year to avail themselves of services there).

The most consistent efforts of lay people to instill liberation theology into Irish Catholic thought and practice have probably come from feminists who fought to resist the Church's patriarchal power in the sexual sphere while maintaining some connection to Christian spirituality. It is therefore no accident that one of Daniel Berrigan's best friends and correspondents in Ireland was feminist theologian Dr Mary Condren.

In August 2002 Condren scheduled the Dublin launch of a new edition of her scholarly classic, *The Serpent and the Goddess*, so that Berrigan could be there to launch it with her, at the Winding Stair bookshop overlooking the River Liffey. Afterward she gave a party for Berrigan in the once-dowdy, now-swishy Clarence Hotel, owned by Irish rock band U2. Rumor had it that Bono himself had got wind that Berrigan was in town and instructed that a room be made available. If so, it was Bono's only known contribution to the anti-war movement in Ireland.

Ireland had made a mark, however, on the global peace and justice movement with disproportionate and powerfully expressed solidarity with Palestine. In 2002 two activists stood out, both of them extraordinarily brave women, neither of them with heavy Catholic baggage. Caoimhe Butterly was young, well-spoken, slightly punky looking with her dyed red hair, and for no reason other than that she couldn't bear injustice had found herself in the Occupied Territories with other young Westerners standing up for the rights of Palestinians. Mary Kelly was a tough, serious, deliberate middle-aged country woman, a nurse, with a long history of left-wing and counter-cultural activity that had taken her from communal life in west Cork to trouble-spots on various continents, from Colombia to Bethlehem.

Butterly had returned from the West Bank with a bullet-wound in her thigh, inflicted by an Israeli soldier in Jenin as she tried to protect children in the midst of a horrible military atrocity. Kelly had also risked her life in May of 2002 to bring supplies to the besieged Palestinians in the Church of the Nativity. Butterly and Kelly had a lot going for them, including credibility and media profile that other activists could only dream of; but they were more likely to be photographed than interviewed, and were rather isolated on the Irish Left, without any strong group behind them. They certainly would not have drawn a crowd of hundreds, let alone thousands, to hear them speak in their home country.

In all these circumstances, it was not clear what combination of solidarity, piety, activism, romance and nostalgia brought so many people out to hear Daniel Berrigan in Dublin. However, what was clear when you thought about Ireland's recent history was that Ciaron O'Reilly, speaking to more than 1,000 people (including his own father who was in Ireland visiting) was nonetheless trying to plant the Dublin Catholic Worker on uncertain and surprisingly inhospitable turf. Liberation theology, despite a flurry of enthusiasm for the Central American variety in the 1980s, had failed to take hold here. And for many leftists, 'Catholic Worker' was an oxymoron, like 'Liberal Fascist'; or perhaps the name evoked some mid-20th-century front group, a Cold War relic used by the church to try to lure the proletariat away from atheistic communism. O'Reilly had a rap that summed up the Catholic Worker's place in the world, or lack thereof: "We are often marginalized as too hip for the straights, too straight for the hips, too fluffy for the spikeys, too spikey for the fluffies, too Christian for the left and too left for the Christians." That might just go double in Ireland.

O'Reilly's own presence in Ireland was itself a result of conflict and contingency, less a mission than a refuge. The late 1990s had been divided for him between England (mainly Liverpool) and Australia, the latter including a large amount of time in jail. The new millennium found him in London, again helping to establish a presence for the Catholic Worker, but also joining the Simon Community, probably the most highly respected, and respectful, of the major organizations providing accommodation and services to homeless people in this part of the world. However, O'Reilly's time there was less than happy: he got into conflict with management when he became very concerned about the death of a volunteer in a Simon hostel. Meanwhile, he was concerned about ongoing surveillance and potential harassment from the British security establishment. When a cousin of his went for a civil-service job and was subject to a routine clearance, Ciaron's name was brought up by the interviewers.

Ciaron had met Dubliner Tom Hyland in course of Timorese solidarity work in the 1990s. Hyland, a bus driver from grey, working-class Ballyfermot in Dublin's western suburbs, had become a national hero in the new state of East Timor for his passionate and tireless solidarity work. In 2002, he was invited to have that status underlined with a hero's welcome from the new government, staffed by many of the exiles he had befriended over the years. Afraid of flying, Hyland was going to need to spend a long time away from home to travel over land and sea to Timor, and to enjoy the hospitality on offer there. Ciaron's interest in coming to Ireland had met Hyland's need for someone to care for his house and dogs while he was away, and the Dublin Catholic Worker was tentatively born when Ciaron arrived in Ballyfermot in April 2002. His old Australian friend and Liverpool Catholic Worker comrade Treena Lenthall was already in Dublin. A further small group of friends he gathered consisted mainly of ex-Catholics. If a Catholic Worker community didn't instantly assemble, the house did become something of a center of activity: Mary Kelly herself stayed with him in Ballyfermot for a few weeks after her return from Palestine.

O'Reilly began to work, as was his custom, with homeless people. And he got quickly down to activist business too: the first Dublin Catholic Worker newsletter was ready for him to hand out at the anarchist May Day 'Reclaim the Streets' demonstration – an event that turned ugly and dispelled any lingering hopes that a diaspora observer such as O'Reilly might have clung to that the cops in Ireland were somehow more sympathetic or less potentially brutal than their American, British or Australian counterparts.

It was quickly apparent that despite the Republic of Ireland's supposed neutrality, there was a significant anti-war agenda to be pursued in the country. Shannon Airport, a facility in County Clare that was a long-time refueling favorite for transatlantic traffic, had been used to move troops and equipment to Afghanistan, in an attack that saw little opposition in Ireland as elsewhere. It was clearly going to play an important part in the next, more controversial war.

A few months before coming to Ireland, Ciaron O'Reilly had his attention directed to Shannon when he got a funny email in England from a Dublin college student, peace activist, and highly useful technology boffin, Eoin Dubsky. Would trespass, Dubsky wondered, count as a Ploughshares action? O'Reilly, a veteran of two indubitable actions seven years and thousands of miles apart, as well as a friend of the all-important Berrigans and the author of two fine books about his experiences in the tradition, was happy to be regarded as capable of offering expert technical opinion on such a question, albeit perhaps with an Americanized slant. He entered into a friendly correspondence with Dubsky, counseling him firmly that, no, trespass was probably not sufficient.

Ploughshares, he said, generally involved a hammer.

Chapter 2

Sowing the Seeds

I T IS NOT WITH ANY GREAT FAITH IN THE INTEGRITY OF POLI-
ticians elsewhere in the world that Irish people tend to regard their
own leaders as among the slipperiest characters ever to put on a
suit. The judgment is not necessarily applied retrospectively through
the history of the State that gained partial independence from Britain
in 1921, then declared itself a Republic in 1949 (leaving the six counties of Northern Ireland under British rule). Indeed the first generations
of freedom-fighters-turned-government-ministers are seen as men
of probity, by and large, whatever their other qualities. The late 20th
century, however, saw the rise of a comfortable and corrupt set of politicians whose self-evident venality was actually supposed to be part of
their post-colonial charm.

Foremost was Charles Haughey, whose many political twists and
turns and strokes of "genius" (Teddy Kennedy's word for him) were
eclipsed, at least in contemporary Irish eyes, by the gradual exposure,
after his retirement in 1992, of the tens of millions of pounds in 'dona-
tions' he solicited from businessmen to maintain a patrician lifestyle,
complete with Georgian country mansion, horses, boats and ownership
of a sizeable and scenic island off the coast of the Dingle peninsula in
County Kerry – even while Ireland continued to languish on Europe's
impoverished fringe. While he was in power, supporters often spoke of
Haughey with a wink and the cliché "better the devil you know…", but
few knew then just how thorough his personal corruption had become
by his final years in office.

In 1997, the office of prime minister ('Taoiseach', in the Irish language) was assumed by Haughey's protégé, Bertie Ahern. An accountant of humble origins, Ahern's 'ordinary' demeanor and almost Bushily error-prone speech patterns, in a working-class Dublin accent, scarcely masked his political skills, including an evasiveness that frustrated opponents and made him an exceptionally successful negotiator. Ahern's personal style was precisely the opposite of Haughey's extravagance – though there eventually were to be public questions about Ahern's own finances, and both his marriage and subsequent long relationship were to suffer public breakdowns. (Haughey had simply conducted widely discussed extramarital affairs.) Haughey had called Ahern the most ruthless and cunning of them all, but unlike Haughey's, Ahern's ruthlessness seemed to be in pursuit of power, pure and simple, not personal pleasure and luxury.

By 2002, Ahern was governing one of the world's most successful economies. The 'Celtic Tiger' had various causes, but it is probably best understood as a consequence of the 'friendly' (i.e. profitable) relationship with the US and multinational business. Attractive tax policies, Bill Clinton's personal interest in the Irish 'peace process' and the American hi-tech and pharmaceutical booms of the 1990s helped establish Ireland as an ideal offshore location for US business: by 2002 nearly a quarter of US investment into the European Union was coming to Ireland. With just four million people, the Republic of Ireland is too small and its Tiger is too complex and contingent (just what would have happened without Viagra in Cork and/or Pentium chips in Kildare?) for it to be held up as a successful model of one form or another of economic development, though that doesn't stop the pundits and politicians of different stripes from citing it either as the model case of low-tax neoliberalism or of government-directed social partnership. Ahern himself occasionally calls himself a 'socialist' – prompting splutters of disbelief across the political spectrum, though it's a clear indication he knows the word still resonates more positively with the populace than it does with the political and media elite. His own public analysis of the Celtic Tiger tended to credit social partnership, not least because he himself has proven so adept at brokering national agreements that govern large sections of the waged economy, with employer and trade-union involvement. This was in keeping with the historic populism of his party, Fianna Fail, tempered in government for most of the recent past by its coalition with the much smaller, right-wing Progressive Democrat (PD) party, who tended to credit neoliberalism, and more specifically themselves, for the historic achievement of a prosperous Ireland.

For all the vaguely leftish populism, however, Ahern was not going to look the American (Trojan?) gift horse in the mouth. Moreover, even after the euphorically warm relations with Bill Clinton had faded from significance – the legendary late Saint Patrick's Night sing-songs in the White House replaced by an annual sober handshake with the dry-drunk Dubya – he and others in the Fianna Fail party would suggest that the relationship with US capital was about more than money, that a supportive political friendship with the United States was broadly in Ireland's interests. (The PDs and the largest opposition party, Fine Gael, unhampered by Fianna Fail's residual populism and unease with imperialism, would express this view rather more directly.)

Ahern's foreign minister was his Fianna Fail party colleague, Brian Cowen, the man most likely to succeed him as Taoiseach. If Ahern had raised political evasiveness and ambiguity to a fine art, then Cowen was at least a master craftsman. Cowen's main failing – apart from notably awful looks, still not regarded as a crippling disability in Irish politics – was his incapacity to indicate convincingly that he believed politics should have anything at all to do with the great unwashed. (His elitism is commonplace; its transparency less so, and only his own down-home, rough rural manner protected him from political damage.) Cowen's every soporific public uttering – muttering, really – carried an implicit message: "leave it to the professionals." Colleagues and journalists encouraged Cowen's arrogance by constantly assuring him, in public and private, that he was the most intelligent and able of all government ministers, that the nation's interests were indeed safe in his hands, that he owed no one any explanations.

These were the shifty characters in charge of Irish foreign policy as the United States suffered the atrocity of the September 11th attacks, then launched the 'War on Terror'. Ireland held a seat on the United Nations Security Council in late 2001 and 2002, and was indeed in the (rotating) presidency in September 2001. Ahern and, especially, Cowen, were four-square behind the US in this period, with Cowen, in early October 2001, praising the Bush administration for its "restraint" in response to 9/11. (That is to say, the Americans had merely locked and loaded, and not yet opened fire on the people of Afghanistan.)

And that's where Shannon comes in. The airport in the west of Ireland, about 100 miles from Dublin, is a remarkably convenient spot for air travellers. To see for yourself, grab a globe and a piece of string and stretch the string from North America to various points in central and eastern Europe, the Middle East and southwest Asia, then look where the middle of the string 'flies' over. Back in Cold War days it was commonplace to see Aeroflot planes, and less often Soviet military ones, stopping in Shannon en route to and from Cuba, even during major East-West crises. Credible rumor had it that would-be defectors at Shannon were told in no uncertain terms that they weren't welcome in Ireland, and manhandled back on to the aircraft. It was nothing personal, or even political; it was strictly business.

The War on Terror, however, was elevating a certain sort of business to unprecedented levels. As early as 2002 there were suspicions that Shannon might be involved in shipping prisoners to Guantánamo; certainly CIA flights stopped there in the course of 'extraordinary rendition' missions, though it is not known if they carried prisoners into and through Ireland. What was beyond dispute was that US troops were passing through Shannon in large and increasing numbers: the famed airport lounges where the creamy whiskey-laced drink known as 'Irish coffee' had been invented a half-century earlier were filling up with soldiers in desert fatigues. Most of the troops were on civilian charter flights, but many military aircraft were also refuelling at the airport. A few horrified locals got out their binoculars and, despite police harassment, began to document the conversion of this civilian airport into a virtual military base: their reports began to appear regularly on the Irish Indymedia website. A grassroots campaign on Shannon swelled in the course of late 2002, as further US war-making looked inevitable.

The Irish government went into slip-sliding mode. In autumn 2002, facing parliamentary questions about what was happening at Shannon, foreign-minister Cowen adopted his typical muttering don't-be-worrying, business-as-usual posture. "There has not been any significant change in the pattern of over flights and landings by foreign military aircraft in recent months," he insisted. It was reminiscent of Richard Pryor's joke about the plea of a man caught *in flagrante* by his wife: "Who you gonna believe, me or your own lyin' eyes?"

Campaigners weren't mollified. Irish law was perfectly clear on these matters: "No foreign military aircraft shall fly over or land in the State save on the express invitation or with the express permission of the minister." Another law prohibits the carrying of "munitions of war" in Ireland except where the minister has given an exemption. Since the government wasn't admitting to giving any such exemption, the overflights and Shannon landings by US troops and craft could only be legal in a rather unlikely set of circumstances: that they were unarmed, carrying no arms, ammunition or explosives and did not form part of a military operation. Cowen told the Irish parliament that he had to accept "in good faith" that these conditions were being met by US flights, and that he wasn't checking.

Of course, in the Dublin government as elsewhere the fiction that there was not a 'military operation' taking place was sustained by the sham of 'negotiating' a solution to the non-existent Iraqi WMD crisis. So Cowen could talk peace: "Ireland wants very much to see a peaceful solution to this crisis. We are working together with the other members of the Security Council to accomplish this objective... The purpose of the UN resolutions is to bring about disarmament. Nothing more." And he could keep the other side of his mouth busy too, with words like this in the UN General Assembly and Irish parliament: "Ireland shares in the growing international consensus that the Iraqi regime poses a potential threat to regional security." In November 2002, speaking to the elite National Committee on American Foreign Policy in New York, Cowen praised America's patience with the UN route and warned: "Iraq must comply. If it does not comply there will be serious consequences." Striking macho postures with high-powered foreign audiences clearly suited Cowen: there was no muttering this time.

Ireland's verbal belligerence about the Saddam Hussein regime was no more morally consistent than that of most other Western countries. When Saddam had been up to least good in the late 1980s, Irish companies had kept his army well fed with plenty of tasty, grass-fed Irish beef – and unloaded a hefty amount of lesser livestock too. This helpful supply line was not simply a matter of the market doing its work. The Irish government, closely aligned with the interests of the beef industry, went to extraordinary and potentially costly lengths to encourage the sale of beef to a potentially risky, war-torn buyer: it earmarked hundreds of millions of dollars, about half of its entire 'Export Credit Insurance' scheme, to guarantee the profits of the particular beef-barons who were targeting the Iraqi market.

With the activity now at Shannon, Ireland's pretension to be a moral actor on the world stage, seen in the tradition of military neutrality and arguably justified by the genuinely independent foreign policy pursued at times from the 1950s (when it supported Chinese membership of the UN) to the 1980s (when Haughey opposed the Falklands war), was exposed in all its cynicism. Neutrality? The Hague convention, later to be cited by an Irish High Court judge, makes a mockery of continuing Irish use of the word. As Justice Kearns wrote: "There is an identifiable rule of customary law in relation to the status of neutrality whereunder a neutral state may not permit the movement of large numbers of troops or munitions of one belligerent State through its territory en route to a theatre of war with another."

So it wasn't just radical-fringe protesters who reckoned there was something rotten in Shannon. But perhaps it was going to have to be such protesters who were prepared to act on their reckoning. In August 2002 Mary Kelly ran on to a runway with a Palestinian flag and anti-war placard. In September Eoin Dubsky settled for something short of Ploughshares and got on to a Shannon runway to spray-paint a massive Hercules transport plane with graffiti: "NO WAR," it said, alongside a peace sign. The police opposed allowing Dubsky out on bail for this rela-tively minor action – though the judge let him go on the condition that he not come within five miles of Shannon Airport while awaiting trial.

Other Irish protests that autumn had an element of civil disobedi-ence, with a few protesters getting to, and through, Shannon Airport's perimeter fence or gathering rather obstructively outside terminal entrances. Ciaron O'Reilly was not centrally involved in most of this activity, but was unavoidably a magnet for a few people determined to step up their protests to a 'higher' level. War was coming. Ireland was complicit. Something had to be done.

One such person was Deirdre Clancy. She was scarcely the most likely recruit to the Catholic Worker; indeed she was not even in attendance at the big August public meeting that had attracted so many people to see and hear Daniel Berrigan. Deirdre was, on the face of it, a success-ful daughter of prosperous Ireland. Born in 1970 into a comfortable, well connected family – though like most Irish families only a couple of generations from peasantry – with her grandfather Sean an honoured member of the freedom-fighting generation who had stood beside Michael Collins as the tricolor flag rose over Dublin Castle, Deirdre had spent most of the 1990s, like so many of her peers, working in and around multinational companies in Ireland's booming high-tech sector.

One of the more liberating aspects of the boom was that people like her could walk in and out of well-paid jobs, in Ireland and abroad, that didn't necessarily tax all their capabilities and also usually didn't force obvious conformity with a buttoned-down corporate culture.

Deirdre, who made her living as an editor, was no ordinary Celtic Tiger cub. As sensitive as she was intelligent, she had been involved in radical, environmental and feminist politics since her teenage years, and was moved to intense sympathy by the suffering of others. By the time she was 16 she felt confidently able to assert and understand that the suffering of the world's poor was no mere tear-jerking accident of nature but the logical consequence of a system of exploitation based in the corporate First World. The horror of war, she came to believe, fit into that system – and her feminist critique of its patriarchal underpinnings was tempered, as for so many feminists at that time, by close observation of the bloodthirsty British prime minister, Margaret Thatcher. Raised a Catholic, for much of her formative late-adolescence and early adulthood Deirdre was an agnostic on matters of religion.

Her student radicalism in the late 1980s and early 1990s at Dublin's elite Trinity College didn't extend to any embrace of the politics of nonviolent direct action. (The continuing violent direct action of the IRA and others at that time invariably clouded the view of such politics.) Deirdre did, however, gain a clear sense of the privileged disconnectedness from reality of most posturing college politicos. The prestigious College Historical Society – the 'Hist', which regularly brings famous guests from around the world to join its 'debates' on all sorts of issues – lost its interest for her by second year, and she resigned from its committee.

It was Iraq that left the most indelible emotional and political mark on Clancy. The first US attack on that country, starting in January 1991, rendered her dumbstruck at the impotence of anti-war politics, which complained incessantly at the media 'sanitising' of the war but scarcely seemed to comprehend just how filthy it was. Her own most abiding media memory of this war was an image of an oil spillage along an Iraqi beach, which was scattered with oil-covered sea birds, still alive, but facing a certain and long-drawn-out death. She figured that if the wildlife and environment were affected in such a way, and it was thought too gory to be shown in detail beyond one extremely brief shot, then the effects on the civilian population of the fireworks display we were subjected to night and day didn't really bear thinking about. But she thought about them constantly.

The sense of impotence, of paralysis, related to herself as much as the wider anti-war movement. Seeking some encouragement, she began to think about the spiritual dimensions of her politics. She was doing a graduate degree in gender and women's studies, and was fortunate to have as a teacher at Trinity a leading feminist theologian, Mary Condren, Condren supervised Clancy's research, and an underlying spirituality became part of the political commitment Deirdre took with her through the 1990s, as she did voluntary work in the area of mental health and visited South Africa, for work purposes, getting a deeper sense of the inequities, and iniquity, of the global capitalist system. She moved to Sweden in 2000, mostly working for Ericsson – the working life turning more unpleasant as high-tech times got tight – but found herself in the US in September 2001 unable to fly out when the airports shut down.

This, she was to write later, "was a turning point that made me realise that peace activism was the only viable option if I was to aspire to a path of integrity.... While I was in awe of the hospitality I received on being stranded in the US at such a charged time, I was also taken aback at some of the reactions to the tragedy I encountered. Having suggested tentatively at a social gathering, at which the causes of the 9/11 attack were being discussed, that US foreign policy may be antagonistic at times, I was met with a shocked silence.... The rest of the evening was spent listening to all the reasons why the assembled company thought there should be heavy bombardment of Afghanistan, and indeed the Middle East generally. Specificities did not appear to matter too much." She returned to Ireland in 2002, after getting a dose of debilitating corporate shenanigans in Sweden, "determined that I would deepen my activism if further unmerited invasions took place."

That was where the Catholic Worker came in. In October, as the national and international arguments grew more insistent, Clancy attended a meeting organised in Dublin by Ciaron O'Reilly. The main speaker was Carmen Trotta, an earnest and warm man from the New York Catholic Worker, a man whose commitment to society's marginalized and to resisting war was matched only by his capacity to imitate Elvis Presley. All these talents were on show as he gigged around Ireland, and Clancy was struck by him and by the clear fit between her own spiritual and political concerns and the philosophy of the Catholic Worker.

By this time O'Reilly was hosting weekly liturgies in Ballyfermot, where politics and spirituality mixed. This was, in some ways, the Catholic Worker movement at its most beautiful, a few people sitting on bare floorboards with a glass of wine and a slice of bread, forging a sense of community. For all the movement's extraordinary services to the poor, and all its tireless resistance to war, there is something about the Catholic Worker 'at home', at prayer, like this that powerfully underlines its spiritual depth. And the spirituality rises up through the small community and engages with the world beyond its walls.

Deirdre began to attend, listening to Ciaron's stories of actions he had taken and supported around the world. One evening she met a small, quiet Scottish highlander who was visiting Ireland: Karen Fallon was a marine biologist, and had worked in that capacity and as a research chemist in her native Scotland and in England, often putting in long laboratory nights. Some of her work, indeed, was covered by Britain's restrictive Official Secrets Act. But while she enjoyed and was good at her work, Karen also saw that science was being used for indefensible purposes, hard-won expertise being exploited by military and governments to hone the tools of death. She had become part of the Trident Ploughshares group, a veteran of actions in Scotland and frequent resident at the Faslane peace camp, where campaigners at a remote sea-side monitored the activities of nuclear-armed submarines and planned actions against them. Karen was arrested more times than she could count or cared to remember; she was told off, fined and incarcerated, but mostly charged and driven home after a cup of coffee and a four-hour processing.

Fallon, who had known Ciaron for about two years, went back to Scotland after just a few October days in Dublin, but promised to stay in touch since he was looking for support in establishing the Dublin Catholic Worker. Karen, raised a Catholic, didn't necessarily see herself in those terms any more, but also didn't see her post-Catholic faith as an insurmountable obstacle: she had, after all, previously helped set up a London Catholic Worker, with Ciaron and others.

Talking to such people, a key insight came to Deirdre Clancy. Perhaps the ability to act courageously and morally against war and war-preparations wasn't the preserve of distant philosophical giants named Berrigan, but could be claimed by anyone – this funny dreadlocked Australian, this tiny squinting Scot, maybe this serious and brainy Dublin editor. She thought too about the tradition of civil disobedience in Ireland, often submerged under the 'physical force' tradition of nationalism, but nonetheless rich and full of courageous women like those involved in the Ladies Land League and the women's suffrage movement. Later she would say: "When you know the truth, sometimes you need to act on that knowledge or go crazy." Sometime late that autumn, Clancy first broached the possibility among the small Dublin Catholic Worker group that they ought to do a Ploughshares action at Shannon.

O'Reilly was not in Ireland with the definite intention of doing any such thing. His role as an inspiration for others was, however, undeniable. In October a TV documentary about O'Reilly and the Catholic Worker went out in RTE TV's Sunday-night religious-programming slot, *Would You Believe*. At a small Catholic seminary in south Dublin, 22-year-old Damien Moran was watching.

Handsome, smart, athletic, Moran was the Irish equivalent of the all-American boy. He was born on July 12th, 1980, and reared smack dab in the boggy middle of the country, in Banagher, County Offaly, where the only tourists you're likely to see are either driving through to the more 'scenic' west or are birdwatchers hoping to spot – or at least hear the famous rattling call of – an elusive corncrake on the nearby Shannon Callows. Barely old enough to remember Ireland's bad old times, Moran was a small-town guy whose father labored 40 years in the state-owned Electricity Supply Board, and whose mother labored equally hard for 40 years at home rearing six children. He had seen his country grow in prosperity, and who'd had enough personal success with girls and on sports fields around Ireland to be full of confidence in his ability to thrive in the wider world.

Ireland is a small island, but it has room for amazing sporting diversity, based on class as well as region. Working-class city and town dwellers (at least in the old British garrison towns) are most inclined toward soccer. Posh boys play rugby – except in and around Limerick, where everyone loves it – and a few better-off Dubliners enjoy field-hockey and cricket. Basketball springs up in the odd suburban working-class estate. However, the broad middle swathe of the Republic's population, especially in rural areas, is intensely loyal to the amateur 'gaelic games', revived from the late 1800s by the Gaelic Athletic Association (GAA) as part of the wider nationalist programme. The GAA and its games are a way of life in Ireland, and indeed in Irish-immigrant communities elsewhere. The games include the most popular, gaelic football, a hard-hitting hand-and-foot game with a superficial resemblance to both soccer and rugby; and the most admired, called 'hurling', a stick-and-ball game played on the same field with similar rules to gaelic football, but with speed and skill, danger and flair, that other games can only dream about, and that television can't quite keep up with.

Hurling, this aristocrat among games, has long been dominated by men from some of Ireland's better-off farming regions – counties

Kilkenny and Tipperary, the northern and eastern part of County Cork, east Galway. It has thrived too in neighbouring areas of Clare, Waterford and Wexford. It had its moments in Dublin, where Deirdre Clancy's father had been a top youth player. But starting in the 1980s, as Damien Moran was growing up in Banagher, the upstart bogmen and townies of County Offaly were challenging the old aristocracy, regularly contesting provincial and national championships – along the way garnering notoriety for their sociable and freewheeling approach to the 'discipline' of elite athletic training. Offaly hurlers knew how to play, and how to party. Young Damien learned fast on both counts.

He captained the under-12 team of his club, St Rynagh's, when they were county champions. Within a couple of years he was working in local pubs, and drinking too. He was, however, also interested in religion – and in a community where any spiritual-interest beyond weekly mumbling mass attendance marked you as something out-of-the-ordinary, this could only mean one thing: he had a 'vocation', a calling, for the priesthood. He allowed the possibility to linger in his teenage mind, as he talked to local priests, and soaked up his Aunt Mary's stories and photographs of life as a nun in Rwanda. When she came home in 1994, having escaped the genocide by virtue of her skin colour, he was horrified and fascinated. He also became fascinated with the history of British oppression in Ireland, and of republican resistance to it. He even tried to organise a school-trip to Belfast, less than 100 miles away but a world apart, where his parents had never been in their lives. However, in the spirit of Augustine, Moran was in no hurry to take on a virtuous life of self-sacrifice: he was in secondary school (equivalent to high school) at a local school full of female boarders, and had every intention of enjoying the opportunities that provided.

He had just turned 17 when he went to college in Galway, and the good life continued. Damien struggled to stay at the very top as a hurler, but in first year he had one of his proudest moments on the pitch: playing defence for University College Galway freshmen, he marked Henry

Shefflin of Waterford Institute of Technology, already seen as one of the most promising forwards in Ireland and destined to be regarded as the first truly great hurler of the 21st century. Before the game started Moran hit Shefflin with the butt of his hurley (stick), spat on him and called his mother a whore. Shefflin failed to score any points from play that day – though Moran's rather-offensive defensive success was not enough to secure victory for his team. And ultimately his determination to make time for his over-active social life, along with his studies and spiritual explorations, meant Damien never played at a much higher level. By his third and final year, the stock answer among his friends to the question "Where's Moran?" was: "Either in the pub drinking or in the cathedral praying." When he finished his final exams in 2000, he skipped the pub and went to an exhibition of Orthodox icons.

He was moving toward a decision on the priesthood, and thought a spell of volunteering abroad would clarify matters. The former principal of his school arranged for him to do volunteer work in Haiti, where her religious order, the La Sainte Union, was active. He worked to raise money for his travels, and to leave behind him in Haiti. On New Year's Eve 2000-2001, he worked in the bar at his uncle's hotel, then went on a three-day bender – the last time he got drunk. His final pint of Guinness was downed two weeks later at Dublin Airport as he set off for the Caribbean. Another two weeks later, at the beginning of Lent, immersed in Haiti's poverty, he 'officially' forswore drink, cigarettes, drugs and sex.

Haiti evangelized Moran, to be sure, but it also radicalized him. Sanctions were bleeding the country. Aristide was back in power, living large in a mansion while his people starved, but the traces of liberation theology in the air had a powerful influence: "Peace in the stomach, peace in the mind," Aristide had said. Damien was struck too by the problems that beset the do-gooders: a hospital negligently allowed TB-infected water to run into a nearby slum via an open ravine – and

Moran observed that at least it was one way to ensure a constant flow of needy patients.

A few months in Haiti were followed by a few more in New York, working illegally as a plumber's assistant. He fixed a luxurious Fifth Avenue shower that his boss insisted belonged to Cindy Crawford, but rather than (just) dwelling on the proximity to carnal greatness, Damien thought of the Haitian sewer. He had dreamed of joining the Jesuits, but the missionary Holy Ghost fathers beckoned, in New York and back in Ireland. Soon he happily started living at their premises in Kimmage, Dublin, in autumn 2001, as Damien first studied at University College Dublin to become a teacher, then started his fast-track seminary studies in earnest the following year. He did teaching-practice at one of Dublin's poshest secondary schools, St Michael's College, and in his first attempt at being a true missionary, he failed abysmally to get the bemused students to take up hurling.

The seminary was no hotbed of radicalism. Most of the other students were Africans, many from relatively elite families with little culture or tradition of dissent, and at any rate little cause to exercise any such tradition in Ireland. One of Damien's best friends was the son of Sierra Leone's post-war justice minister. Kimmage did, however, also host a small development-studies college, and its students were rather more socially engaged. Moran was quickly involved with them in setting up an Amnesty branch, protesting against Guantánamo and learning from Eoin Lambert, a Holy Ghost priest who had been expelled from Ethiopia by the Vatican for cultivating close ties with Muslims and Orthodox Christians to cooperate against AIDS.

In the midst of his spiritual and political commitments, however, Moran had another concern: Dorota, a beautiful Polish woman he had met in Paris during the summer of 2002. Now far more sober and chaste than the stereotypical Irishman, Moran was nonetheless charming and, with his guitar, had won her heart over the course of his 22nd birthday evening in 'Le Pub Galway'. Their bond didn't stray beyond the spiritual

– just as well, since he had been staying in Paris with Holy Ghost fathers near the Pantheon – but the relationship was a powerful distraction even when he got back to Kimmage.

Unlike Deirdre Clancy, Moran had little familiarity with the specific tradition of the Catholic Worker until he saw Ciaron O'Reilly on TV. It struck home immediately. He scribbled down the email address given at the end of the programme and got in touch with Ciaron. On November 16th there was to be a protest (small, as usual) at the US embassy against the notorious military training camp, the School of the Americas. Moran offered to make a banner, and on a chilly day in south Dublin he brought it along and met O'Reilly for the first time. He met him again a week later at a public meeting when O'Reilly spoke alongside Shannon plane-spotter Tim Hourigan, Shannon graffiti-artist Eoin Dubsky and Dublin Indymedia activist Chekov Feeney.

"I'm up for something," Moran quietly told Ciaron, though the young man didn't initially make much of an impression on the older activist.

Nonetheless, Moran and Deirdre Clancy were both clearly "up for something." So too, possibly, was Dave Donnellan, another friend who had discovered the group at the same public meeting. The possibility of a group Ploughshares action was now very real, the subject of a great deal of sincere prayer and reflection. Ciaron, Deirdre, Damien and Dave, with some others, visited Shannon, attending an anti-war rally there on December 11th. Ciaron, aware of the US Plowshares tradition whereby you do minor arrestable actions first as part of your preparation for a big event, led five others wading into one of those typical pieces of airport art, a fountain with an abstract but clearly aeronautical piece of sculpture in the middle of it. They put red dye in the fountain and daubed the sculpture, "The War Stops Here. Phil Berrigan, RIP" – the great Plowshares pioneer and friend of Ciaron's had died just a few days earlier.

But the water was cold, there was a protest to police, and the cops, though they ran to the poolside, couldn't bother themselves to wade in after the Catholic Worker contingent and cuff them for this spot of vandalism. The arrests would have to wait for another day.

Chapter 3

The Spirit Moves

WHEN LOCAL ANTI-WAR CAMPAIGNERS WEREN'T OUT at the airport, watching and protesting, some of them were paying visits to the local Garda (police) station, in the tiny town of Shannon nearby. Repeatedly they told the local cops that they believed illegal activity – essentially the presence of uniformed troops and munitions – was taking place at the airport, and that gardaí (the plural form in the Irish language) should inspect and investigate. One of the frequent 'complainers' was a silver-haired former Irish army commandant, Edward Horgan, but not even Ed's eminently respectable status could make the police take much notice in the face of the Irish government's see-no-evil policy, and the public complaints were filed away.

The cops' willful ignorance was dramatized to amusing effect in mid-December 2002, when Eoin Dubsky was brought to trial in a local court near the airport for his September paint-job on a US military-transport plane. Dubsky argued that he had a 'lawful excuse' for the damage he had done, and tried to focus the juryless court's attention on what, precisely, the US was doing with all these flights through Shannon. The Indymedia reporter captured the occasion:

> Even though many of the prosecution witnesses admitted that they had NO IDEA what was carried on these flights, Inspector Kennedy of Shannon Garda Station (prosecuting), tried to assure the judge that he was sure that there was nothing untoward.
>
> He assumed that the aircraft were carrying "logistical supplies".

> Judge Mangan asked Inspector Kennedy what "logistical sup-
> plies" were.
> "Equipment," replied Inspector Kennedy.
> The judge just looked at him.
> "Well, I assume they carry American food to their troops."
> "So, you think they're carrying hamburgers?" asked the judge.
> I didn't quite hear Inspector Kennedy's answer due to the laugh-
> ter in the courthouse.

For many local people, however, the goings-on at Shannon Airport
were no laughing matter. A few trivial confrontations between police
and protesters during that autumn had been wildly inflated by the local
and national media, and the anti-protest rantings of a few local politicians helped to embed a caricature of protesters as dangerously violent.
Moreover, protest was often described as a risk to the local economy,
potentially costing Shannon not only the US military traffic but damage
to its reputation, especially among key US customers. An 'enterprise
zone' near the airport had long offered attractive terms to American
companies; about 60 per cent of investment in the Shannon region was
from the US, a government minister said.

The reality was that Shannon Airport was indeed vulnerable economically, but it was fundamentally because of Irish government policy
rather than protest – making it all the more important that politicians
deflect attention on to the anti-war movement.

In general, Shannon's desirability for transatlantic civilian flights had
diminished in recent years because of the increased long-haul capacity of many craft, which no longer needed to touch down at this first
ocean-side landfall. However, the airport's status had been protected by
the state's policy of the 'Shannon stopover', which required carriers that
wanted to fly into Ireland to serve Shannon. The stop was long regarded as something of a headache by Dublin-based or Dublin-bound air
travelers, who often had to endure early-morning hours in Shannon's
sickly-orange transit lounge; but for as long as a high proportion of
Irish-bound transatlantic traffic consisted of tourists and roots-hunters

heading for the west of the country, it made a certain amount of sense not only for regional development but for airlines and passengers. By the 1990s, however, the Dublin region contained one of the world's fastest-growing economies, and the 'stopover' rule was relaxed to facilitate a higher proportion of direct flights between Dublin and North America. By the early 21st century, with the European Union having embraced an aggressive policy of neo-liberalism, it was evident that the Irish government would eventually approve the EU's 'Open Skies' and entirely eliminate the regulations that helped keep Shannon busy.

Of course it was easier and more politically expedient to blame Shannon's troubles on anarchist punks and long-hairs than to question the shibboleths of neo-liberalism or the commitment of the government to sharing the benefits of the Celtic Tiger around the regions. Many anti-war protesters didn't help matters by contrasting their higher morality with the economic 'greed' of locals who wanted to keep the refueling business at Shannon. The fact was that, in and of itself, except for companies such as Top Oil that were directly involved in servicing the US military planes and troop charters, the military-refueling stop wasn't particularly good business, particularly since the government was waiving many of the usual fees for these American flights.

Locals were never as universally hostile to protest as the media pretended, but neither were the environs of the airport, and even the city of Limerick a half-hour up the road, fertile ground for a strong indigenous campaign against the US military at Shannon.

Back on the national stage, Ireland slithered off the UN Security Council at the end of 2002, the expiration of its term being very timely for a government that wanted to continue talking out of both sides of its mouth. Brian Cowen, when he wasn't tough-talking about Saddam, kept describing the Shannon facility for the US military as business as usual, telling parliament on January 13th, 2003. "Shannon is one of a number of European airports used for many years as a transit by US aircraft, mainly for the transit of military personnel to a wide range of destinations. It appears that Shannon is chosen by the US because it offers quick turn-around with efficient and friendly service." Friendly, indeed.

By this time it was clear a large proportion of the Irish public wasn't buying his line. Over the Christmas and New Year's holidays the topic suddenly turned into a major talking point in the media. And on the painfully cold night of Saturday January 4th, a small group of women initiated a campaign tactic that helped capture the public imagination and made Shannon the focus of the media debate: they started a 'peace camp' on the airport grounds. Originally dubbed a "women's peace camp" and set to last just a couple of days – 'Women's Christmas', widely celebrated by Irish feminists, fell on the following Monday – it included some seasoned activists: Mary Kelly was there, and so was Margaretta D'Arcy, a Galway-based artist and activist whose modes of resistance over the years had ranged from radical theatre in London to Greenham Common to pirate radio and beyond.

By Monday the camp had decided to stay. A student-camper went on Indymedia to call for reinforcement:

> Everyone is welcome to the camp, your support is desperately needed, whether male, female, neither or both! If you are against a war in Iraq ignited by George W. Bush, if you are against the killing of innocent civilians, if you are against the use of Shannon Airport and the Irish state's complicity in this military aggression, COME TO THE SHANNON PEACE CAMP. While the weekend vigil was initiated by women it was sustained by all. It would not have been possible to remain in -7 degree temperatures [that's Celsius, about 20 degrees F.] on the first night without the constant supply of hot food, firewood and well wishing by local men, women and children and the lads involved in peace camp. So I say now the momentum is there, we can all give something to the sustaining of the camp.

The Shannon Peace Camp duly gained a more permanent presence; Ed Horgan and a clean-cut local activist-turned planespotter named Tim Hourigan were the most visible among the men who joined in and made it a base. One man from the nearby town, Conor Cregan, was also among the most valuable and useful activists. For the next month, the camp, though often sustained by just a handful of people, became a magnet for activism and media attention.

The Irish Anti-War Movement (IAWM), most active 100 miles east in Dublin where it was largely controlled by the Socialist Workers Party (SWP), did not have an obvious role in the foundation of the camp. However, it had been organizing steadily growing anti-war demonstrations for months, attracting more mainstream political players to the cause, and its spokespeople were seasoned campaigners. Thus as attention turned to the impending war and to Shannon, IAWM chairman and SWP member Richard Boyd-Barrett – young, attractive, articulate – became the ubiquitous face and voice of anti-war politics in Ireland. On the Friday after the camp was established, Ireland's most popular TV program, *The Late Late Show* (which strangely goes out at a mere 9.30pm), devoted a long segment to discussing the issues. Peace Campers Mary Kelly and Tim Hourigan made contributions from the studio audience, but pride of place onstage went to Boyd-Barrett and his IAWM/SWP colleague, Aoife Ní Fheargaill – also young, attractive and articulate. Most anti-war people were delighted with the programme and the performances, but among some of the non-IAWM 'movement', there was some resentment expressed at what was perceived as piggybacking, at best, and poaching, at worst, by elements that hadn't been involved at Shannon. As the month of January 2003 went on and in radio and TV shows and newspaper interviews the IAWM allowed itself to be presented as the de facto movement (its presumptious name rather underlining that impression), speaking for all the activity at Shannon, the tensions grew.

Back in Dublin, Ciaron O'Reilly had just started work at a 'wet shelter', where homeless alcoholics were, unusually, permitted to drink on the premises. Meanwhile, the Dublin Catholic Worker 'movement' was slowly gathering adherents, or at least friends. On New Year's Day Nuin Dunlop arrived, unannounced, at the house in Ballyfermot. Of

Irish extraction, her black hair and blue eyes evoked the classic Irish 'combination', but the high cheekbones and somber expression spoke more directly of her native-American ancestry, as did her slow, flat, careful way of talking. Her striking manner was also a product of her upbringing, which took her from an early childhood in the Appalachian regions of Ohio and West Virginia to a life lived mainly, and through many moves, around the American West. Just over 30 years old, Nuin had lived and worked in Catholic Worker communities in San Francisco and Denver. With a degree in psychology and another one in theology, she had worked doing counselling – and some 'chaplaincy' – in the US for a decade. Dunlop had many years of experience with people who had HIV and AIDS, and also worked for time in Colorado in a Native American women's centre. She was a serious, generous and beautiful activist, and had never put herself in serious trouble with the law.

That winter she was living briefly in Scotland, where she met Karen Fallon. At the Faslane naval base that season, Karen and Nuin had been especially well placed to see that, for all the talk of diplomatic solutions, the British and US military machines were being oiled for war. More ships were going in and out from the harbor, and helicopter traffic was thick overhead. Jets were flying by further above. Nearly every morning at the Faslane peace camp, campaigners were awakened by gunfire from the firing range in the hills near the shore. In December the HMS Ark Royal, a 700-foot aircraft carrier, arrived in the area. Activity had steadily increased for weeks, and by the turn of the year it seemed positively frantic.

When Nuin expressed an interest in going to Ireland, Karen gave her Ciaron O'Reilly's address. Nuin wasn't just looking for a vacation. She wanted to do something about the coming war, and she hoped to find a community in Ireland with which to do it.

Nuin's New Year visit lasted only a couple of days before she headed back to Scotland, but she was in Ireland long enough for Ciaron to tell her about the Dublin Catholic Worker and some of its plans; Nuin – though she came from the less direct-action-oriented western-US outposts of the Catholic Worker – made it clear she was prepared to act. While Eoin Dubsky was still awaiting a verdict from his December hearing (and was also pursuing other legal routes against the government), Ciaron had also already discussed direct-action with Mary Kelly, and Caoimhe Butterly was considering her options.

If plan-making like this remained a fringe activity, it was clearly a fringe that was thick with highly principled and solid people, and those people in turn were making friends near Shannon such as Conor Cregan, Ed Horgan and Tim Hourigan.

While Boyd-Barrett led the arguments against the war *per se*, for much of January Horgan and Hourigan made some of the media running that was specific to Shannon – and to what the government wasn't telling about US 'business' there. From broadcasters' point of view they were good characters, with country accents and turns of wry humour to go with their encyclopedic knowledge and spotting scopes. Hourigan turned up on RTE's main current-affairs programme, *Prime Time*, where foreign-minister Brian Cowen was protected from a live debate with him. On national radio a reporter followed him around the airport as he pointed out US military craft and was harassed by the airport police. He and Horgan repeatedly contacted the local police to report what they believed to be planes carrying heavy munitions, unauthorized, unreported and without special security escort. Hourigan posted copiously on to the Indymedia site, virtually plane by plane. As footage appeared of uniformed troops in the airport, the government eventually made the small, obvious acknowledgment that soldiers' light-arms were passing through Shannon, and, uh, that was all right now because we say so.

The various strands of anti-war politics in Ireland came together at Shannon on January 18th 2003, when the IAWM called a demonstration there on a 'worldwide day of action'. The turnout, probably about 3,000 people, was roughly five times bigger than any of the previous Shannon protests, and up there with the best that had been managed in Dublin in 2002. The anti-war movement had momentum. And the Catholic Worker group was there: Damien Moran, just back from a 'skiing holiday' in Poland – his thin pretext for getting to see Dorota, to cement the reality of their romance and to warn her of what was coming for him – had adapted his anti-School of the Americas banner to denounce the airport's role in war-making.

Ciaron O'Reilly had his doubts about the effectiveness of such demonstrations, but he was certainly impressed by the mobilization. Even at well over six feet tall he was having trouble getting a full visual sense of the assembly and, looking around, he decided to check out the view from a nearby airport building. He went up on to a rooftop, and was joined by a small group of other people, several of them young anarchists with scarves wrapped across their faces to hide their identities. Suddenly O'Reilly realized he was at the center of an accidental 'occupation', his height and dreadlocks making him look like the figurehead behind this bold radical move – one that diverted the attention of much of the gathered crowd from the familiar ritual of chants and speeches taking place below.

By this time most people believed a new attack on Iraq was imminent, perhaps coming in early February. As part of a group now committed to some sort of more substantial action as soon as possible, Ciaron wasn't planning to do a prolonged airport occupation, and there was relief all around when the rooftop protest petered out and that day's thousands of demonstrators started what was for most of them the long journey home to various corners of Ireland.

Meanwhile, on the other side of the fence, US troops were pouring through Shannon at a rate of nearly 1,000 per day.

Back in Dublin, the Catholic Worker group continued to take coherent shape. Ciaron had written to Nuin Dunlop and Karen Fallon in Scotland: they were prepared to discuss an action and would land in Ireland on Friday, January 24th. Caoimhe Butterly was hoping to take part. Dave Donnellan was also aboard, though he was going to be on a previously planned trip abroad in late January. The prospect of a Shannon Seven was real. But the precise shape of their activity was still uncertain. There were a number of people, from the US, Britain, Ireland and elsewhere, who were planning to travel to Iraq – the peacemakers who became known as the 'human shields', though they were well aware that their presence could scarcely offer much protection. Would the Dublin Catholic Worker group be better-off doing something like that, rather than seeking a war-preparation 'target' in Ireland?

Their reflections were to be aided by the brief presence in Ireland of one of the global peace-and-justice movement's most trusted and indeed beloved activists, Kathy Kelly. A founder of Voices in the Wilderness, Kelly had been in prison many times and Iraq more often again: she was on the way to the latter place now as the mooted tactic of 'Shock and Awe' loomed large.

Kelly was in Ireland to take part in a conference, 'Pathways to Peace', organized by a unique Irish NGO called Action from Ireland (AfrI), a peace and human rights group with a Third World orientation and, unusually, a real fighting spirit at home. In 2001, for example, it had campaigned against the Irish government's referendum to ratify the EU's Nice Treaty – a formula for closer EU integration that underlined the union's growing neo-liberalism, threatened to marginalize smaller states and could bring 'neutral' Ireland closer to a new European military formation. Shockingly for Europe's and Ireland's elites, lined up almost unanimously behind the treaty, the 'No' vote won. (The government insisted on a re-run in 2002 and with some complicated promises on neutrality it secured a victory, though the whole episode remained indicative of popular sentiment against foreign military entanglements.) AfrI, and its annual conference in Kildare, about 30 miles from Dublin, personified a peculiarly Irish tradition of left-internationalism, with support from a few old missionaries and other religious and lay Catholics who had quietly carried a strain of liberation theology home from the developing world, and had found little other way of giving it expression.

The AfrI conference occurs each year as part of a festival in Kildare called Féile Bríde, or the Brigid's Festival. St Brigid of Kildare, whose feast day falls on February 1st, supposedly lived and founded a powerful convent in the 5th and 6th centuries, making her a contemporary of St Patrick, and second only to him as patron of Ireland. The Brigid's Cross, usually homemade out of reeds, is a much-loved national and familial token in Ireland. But the tale of the saint is also complicated by the fact that Brigid is the name of one of the great goddesses of pre-Christian Irish mythology, who had power over fire and was supposed to have had a sanctuary at Kildare. Whether Brigid the saint was a real individual or a fictitious figure employed to Christianize a potent local cult – or indeed something in between – remains a matter of controversy. What is certain is that in the late 20th century, she became a focus for a somewhat New-Agey 'Celtic' spirituality in Ireland, and her festival a particularly attractive gathering point for women seeking religious resonance a little, but not too far, outside the confines of traditional Catholicism.

Thus every year AfrI gathers in a rambling, slightly worn, mid-20th-century school building in Kildare town, and the political activists are joined by hundreds of people, overwhelmingly middle-aged women – including the locally based Brigidine sisters (not Brigid's own convent but a 19th-century revival of it). Before the speeches, the day begins with a ceremonial flame being placed in "the sacred space".

On January 25th, 2003, into this extraordinary, almost subterranean mélange of action and faith, of Christian and pagan, a realm hardly seen in official portraits of 21st-century Ireland, walked Deirdre Clancy, Nuin Dunlop, Karen Fallon, Damien Moran and Ciaron O'Reilly. They heard Kathy Kelly speak to the assembly, and spoke to her privately afterward. Kelly's empathy with the fearful Iraqi people was extraordinary, and so was her mastery of Iraqi matters in general – she had lived in Iraq for nearly three months before Christmas. It became clear to the new Dublin Catholic Worker group that for them to travel to Iraq for the first time on the eve of war, with no knowledge of Arabic, might do more harm than good for the people they wished to support and protect. Visas, Kelly told them, would be very hard to come by. Kelly's message was that the war against the Iraqi people had been going on continuously since 1991. She gave the group some laminated photographs of Iraqi children.

The first photograph, taken in 1996 by Rick McDowell of Voices in the Wilderness, showed a smiling little girl who was exceptional because she was able to go home from the hospital, healthy after successful treatment in a struggling Iraqi facility.

The next photo showed six-year-old Noor, who suffocated under debris when a US bomb intended for a fertilizer factory hit her street in the Jumurriyah neighbourhood of Basra on January 25th, 1999, a neighbourhood where Kelly lived in 2000. The photo was taken by Nebil Al Jorani, a photographer working for a hotel in Basra. He was hired to photograph tourists, Kelly explained, but there weren't many tourists in Basra at that time.

The third photograph, taken on the same day by the same photographer, showed Noor's father holding the limp and lifeless body of another of his children. This photo was also taken on January 25th, 1999 by Nebil Al Jorani.

The last two photographs were of children in an advanced stage of malnutrition. One showed a doctor pinching a child's flesh to show how it fell from her bones.

Kelly reminded the Kildare gathering of Madeleine Albright's infamous 1996 phrase about the deaths of hundreds of thousands of Iraqi children: "We think the price is worth it." And she reminded them that Albright was promoted to Secretary of State the following year.

The AfrI conference climaxed on the Saturday evening, as usual, with an Irish-dancing session, a céilí – with inevitable multicultural twists. Caoimhe Butterly, who had been speaking that afternoon about her experiences in the Occupied Territories, was along to dance, with a Palestinian friend who had been one of the PLO fighters under Israeli siege in the Church of the Nativity. He had been granted refuge in Ireland in the deal that ended the stand-off. Ciaron O'Reilly chatted with the man, who was named Jihad, and typically couldn't resist joking with him that the name must pose a few problems at passport-control points.

Back in Ballyfermot by Sunday afternoon, it was time for the group to get down to the business of preparing for an action at Shannon. Damien Moran had a little Honda 50 motor scooter, and ran it around Ballyfermot and out to the highway-side hardware stores looking for the tools of the trade – wire cutters, hammers large and small etc. Locked out of the house on one occasion, he knocked on the next-door neighbour's door and left in her keeping a huge gardening mattock – like a pickaxe, with one end sharp but the other broad, useful for uprooting large plants. The neighbour, somewhat bemused, held on to it until Ciaron came home and collected it.

As fate would have it, Tom Hyland's ship came in from East Timor around this time, and he returned to his home after most of a year away to find it full of plotting strangers, mysterious long-haired women using soldering irons to inscribe slogans and quotes into the wooden handles of hammers. Hyland had always balanced his work, and public image, as an activist with a friendly at-home 'ordinariness' that he felt his neighbours would appreciate. He would certainly not condemn the plans of the activists who had taken over his home, whatever those plans might be, but not surprisingly, he seemed to feel his good-neighbourliness could be threatened by the goings-on of Ciaron O'Reilly and company. It was time for the Dublin Catholic Worker to move on.

Damien Moran went home to Banagher, in search of a lump-hammer. The tool in question was a funny sort of family heirloom. Some 14 years earlier, when Damien was still just a wee lad, he and his family had driven up to Dublin in their old Ford Cortina to see Offaly in a big hurling match at Croke Park, the great hulking GAA stadium on the northside of the capital. While they were at the game, the car was stolen. Eventually the police found it, abandoned in the furthest south-west corner of Dublin, in Tallaght. And lying on the seat was the weapon that had been used to smash its window and gain entry. Now, many years later and on the verge of committing an act that, however justified he believed it to be, was probably going to put him on the wrong side of the authorities, Damien felt a strange compulsion to connect himself with the undoubtedly poor young man, the ordinary criminal, who had stolen the Moran family's car. He wanted to use his lump-hammer.

Back in Banagher his mother didn't know about the hammer, and didn't know what Damien had in mind, but clearly it was connected to the protests at Shannon. As he left the house she called out a warning to him: "Whatever you do, don't get in trouble with the law. It'll look bad on your CV."

Damien, tense and torn between his genuine respect for his parents' moral compass and his readiness for action he knew they would not support if he told them, found himself enraged by this small-town calculus, and was momentarily the adolescent bad boy again, rather than the seminarian mammy's pet. "Fuck my CV!" he shouted.

Back in Dublin Ciaron O'Reilly was watching *The Simpsons* and freaking out at the sight of Sideshow Bob, tall and sort-of dreadlocked, working on an air base (of all places) as part of a prison work detail. It was time to go on retreat.

Caoimhe Butterly was away in London by now, but still potentially involved in the forthcoming action. Dave Donnellan had come back from abroad and discovered that in a week of intense preparation, including the crucial AfrI conference, the others had moved so far along toward action that in his heart he couldn't catch up. He told the group he would give logistical support rather than take direct action himself. That, crucially, meant driving, and while Damien Moran made his way west from Banagher, Dave drove the other four certain participants, O'Reilly, Deirdre Clancy, Nuin Dunlop and Karen Fallon, to Glenstal Abbey in Murroe, County Limerick.

Glenstal Abbey, which Dave had booked for all six of them, had the dual attraction of being less than an hour from Shannon Airport, close enough to strike whenever the opportunity was right, and offering facilities for a group retreat, under the direction of kind and genuine monks. The Benedictine monastery is in a beautiful location, with part of the premises located within the walls of a Norman-style 'castle' – actually just a low-slung big house built by the old Anglo-Irish landlords in the 19th century. There the Catholic Worker group could talk among themselves, get guidance from the accommodation master, Brother Ambrose, and their own retreat advisor, Brother Anthony. They also attended liturgies and silent mealtimes with the brothers at the long monastery tables. But it was not all spiritual peace: Nuin was getting visibly nervous, and so was Ciaron, often waking up the others to hold 'emergency meetings.'

Damien Moran, in general, didn't take much part in the days of prayerful reflection and nervous talking at Glenstal. He was busy, day and night, at the airport, walking the fences and riding around on his bicycle, casing the joint. Late on the night of Tuesday, January 28th, he was getting a guided look-around the place from Mary Kelly, who was still a stalwart of the Shannon Peace Camp. The atmosphere was fevered, the newspapers had been full of the prospects of war, the UN talking-shop looking increasingly useless. It was a quiet night at the peace camp, but a busy one out on the runways.

Kelly and Moran, walking around in the glow of the airport lights, met Tim Hourigan, the trusted and tireless planespotter. (Hourigan's skills at identifying craft had been self-taught in recent months, as he was quick to assure people who wondered if he had always been a binoculared nerd.) "Do you know what's there parked just off the runway?" Tim said, with some excitement. "It's a C-40 logistics plane, with US Navy markings – a Boeing 737 converted for military transport." He pointed it out to Kelly and Moran.

"Right," Kelly said. "I'm going to get it."

And Mary Kelly was away. Her friends left standing by the perimeter fence didn't know she had already bought a hatchet for just such a moment. She had gone over the fence already, with her Palestinian flag, in August. It was no great strain to her to get past it again, this time bringing the hatchet and using it on the nose of the plane before being arrested. It was an extraordinary embarrassment for the authorities, who had been assuring the public that there was no security risk at the airport – only to see security breached by a militant middle-aged nurse who had been encamped there under their noses for most of the last month.

Kelly's quick-thinking solo action also posed problems for the Catholic Worker group, less because Kelly had stolen their potential thunder than because they would now have to face considerably stepped-up security if they were going to manage to carry out an action. Back at Glenstal they began to think their ambitions would have to be curtailed.

And back in Ballyfermot, Tom Hyland's neighbour saw Mary Kelly's picture on TV and in the *Evening Herald*. She remembered the face from Kelly's spell next-door some months previously. Then she remembered the enormous axe she had been asked to mind by young Damien Moran. Could her own fingerprints be on Mary Kelly's axe?

She needn't have worried. The cops had their woman, and weren't looking for another one. The media frenzy, some of it labeling Kelly as a sympathizer with Irish-republican 'terrorists', was beginning. The Sunday *Independent* – Ireland's top-selling paper and the main press cheerleader for war – concluded, bizarrely, that a US Navy transport plane has "zero military application". The paper's 'journalist', Brendan O'Connor, helpfully visited the craft and explained that the poor old plane, the 'City of Dallas', was harmlessly en route to "an Italian airbase at Sigonella near Naples, a NATO logistics base." In fact Sigonella contains the US Navy's crucial 'hub of the Med' – O'Connor studiously avoided the word Mediterranean lest some readers recall that a sea of that name is adjacent to the Middle East. And furthermore, Sigonella is in Sicily – "near Naples" in the way that Cape Cod might be said to be "near Philadelphia".

Meanwhile, it was announced that the Irish army was being brought in to secure the airport. Arguments about 'direct action' began to rage inside and outside the movement. The peace camp mostly stood behind Kelly publicly, but privately divisions were emerging. Camper Tracy Ryan told the *Irish Times* that people there should "take a non-direct-action" pledge. AfrI planned a demonstration at Shannon on Saturday, February 1st, but it was clear the numbers weren't going to be anything like those of two weeks earlier. Shannon was suddenly a little scary.

In a Limerick monastery, five people wondered what they would do next.

Chapter 4

Getting Airborne

MARY KELLY WAS IN JAIL IN LIMERICK, CHARGED WITH criminal damage and trespass, her small axe filed in the evidence cupboard at Shannon Garda Station. The wounded 'City of Dallas', with its Texas-shaped insignia, was put under police protection and moved to a hangar marked 'SRS', where pictures of the damage Kelly had done were sent by video satellite link to Kansas and the emergency repairs that would allow it to limp home could begin. The Catholic Worker group was still reflecting in Glenstal Abbey, and coming to the decision that they would proceed with their own plans and tools, though they were less hopeful about reaching any significant target.

Ciaron O'Reilly had some particularly significant tools in his kit bag, from the important standpoints of ritual and tradition. Two good-sized hammers dated back to his part in the Anzus Ploughshares action in upstate New York on New Year's Day 1991. One of those two hammers he had parted with on three further occasions over the subsequent decade so that other people could use them in disarmament actions in Britain: members of the BAE Ploughshares (1993), Seeds of Hope Ploughshares (1996) and Jubilee Ploughshares (2000) had all wielded it, then later reclaimed it from the police boxes.

For all of O'Reilly's devotion to what he saw as a rather sacred inheritance, however, humour was never far away. Weeks earlier he had been in Dublin's broad central avenue, O'Connell Street, and seen in one of the tourist shops a six-foot-long inflatable hammer, garishly decked in green, white and orange and carrying the slogan "Hammered by the Irish". Its main purpose in life, if it could be said to have one, was to be borne to international soccer matches and deployed with mock threat in the direction of Ireland's opposition.

It was irresistible. In fact, O'Reilly bought a few of them and posted them off to friends as encouragement for action. Karen Fallon particularly loved the thought of bringing one into Shannon and, after all the stories about stepped-up security in the wake of Mary Kelly's action, she hoped the sight of a big balloon bouncing along in the arms of a tiny woman might just discourage armed guards from shooting first and asking questions later. Having proven to her assembled colleagues that she was uncannily fast at blowing up this toy, Karen earned the right to carry a 'hammer' that when inflated was bigger than herself.

By this time, Deirdre Clancy could scarcely believe that, on their first meeting a few months earlier, she had taken Karen for a shy and retiring type. Fallon was boisterous, funny and smart, the quintessential hard-bitten Scot, well able to enjoy a few drinks and to fight for what she believed in. "Ah tell ya, man" punctuated her conversation, and it brooked no argument. She could justify her actions with politics, philosophy and theology if called upon, but was just as likely to cut to the chase with a profanity: "I don't give a fuck what anyone else thinks." ("Anyone else," in a statement like that, was likely to be the war-accepting world outside, not friends and comrades, with whom she usually settled differences more amicably. Eventually.)

It was getting near the time to act. Apart from their reading of the geopolitical situation, the five were going to lose their car and driver: Dave Donnellan would have to return to Dublin eventually. Dave's car, a low-slung Nissan Micra, was, in any case, a little short of the ideal group transport even for the short runs between Glenstal Abbey and Shannon Airport: it couldn't even carry a full load over the speed-bumps in the abbey's driveway.

"Fuck it, Ah'll go in the boot," Karen had said the first time they all tried to squeeze in, and Karen-in-the-trunk became standard operating procedure. Thus many top-secret conversations about strategy and tactics were shouted at full volume in that car so that Karen, curled up in the back of the vehicle, could take part.

On Friday night's Late Late Show on RTE TV, meanwhile, Minister for Transport Seamus Brennan stated twice that with security increased, there could not possibly be a repeat of the Mary Kelly incident.

At Glenstal Abbey that night, the would-be Ploughshares were ready to act, just waiting for word of a suitable target at the airport. On Saturday morning, February 1st, St Brigid's Day, Dave drove the five down to Clare for the AfrI demonstration – which took the form of a five-mile walk from the tourist attraction of Bunratty Castle to Shannon Airport. As the Catholic Worker group drove along to the event, however, a plane was seen on the tarmac at the airport – one of the most distinctive craft in the US Air Force armory. Even to those unschooled in military trivia, it was hard to mistake an AWACS (for 'airborne warning and control system'), with its extraordinary rotating black radar dome, 30 feet in diameter, six feet thick and suspended weirdly 14 feet above the body of the plane, not far from its tail. This was an E-3 Sentry, and its duties in Afghanistan and its likely ones in Iraq were very serious indeed, though the *Sunday Independent* might conclude that since it would not drop bombs it had "zero military application". While other planes were performing bombing missions, the AWACS would fly high and act as what Tim Hourigan called "a flying air traffic control centre," directing pilots to targets. As a symbol, and a real instrument, of America's deadly and technologically sophisticated application of 'air power' you could hardly find a more potent piece of equipment.

The circumstances, however, were slightly complicated. It was broad daylight, and hundreds of peace campaigners, many of them in family groups, were coming up the road to the airport. Former UN assistant secretary-general Denis Halliday was among them. He was the Irishman who was United Nations 'Humanitarian Coordinator' in Iraq in 1997-98, at the rank of UN assistant secretary-general. He resigned that post in protest at economic sanctions in 1998, and had been a powerful advocate for the Iraqi people since then. Halliday's experience, and his articulate, forensic and not terribly diplomatic dissection of UN and US policy, made a deep impression on those who heard him, including the five; he was doing a lot of writing, public speaking and media appearances at this time.

So he was speaking, and Luka Bloom was going to sing songs. Would it be appropriate to attack a plane in a situation where this highly law-abiding demonstration, with its inevitable horses-and-helicopter police escort, might then be viewed as having provided cover, a 'decoy' for the real business of attacking military property?

The consensus-based 'conference' in Dave's car didn't take long to decide. Would they go for the AWACS? Karen shouted and knocked her assent from the boot of the car. The rest of them agreed. They drove right past the peace walk, to the bewilderment of friends taking part, and on to the airport, heading for a place where they could get near the spot on the seven-mile perimeter fence that Damien had already identified as sufficiently hidden and vulnerable for such a mission.

Unfortunately, the AWACS was a moving target: they had barely got there and begun inventorying their materials when with a roar and a whoosh the refueled plane took off again into the Irish sky. It was an opportunity missed: while there wasn't exactly a shortage of military hardware coming through the airport, most of the flights being objected to were more prosaic passenger aircraft chartered from civilian companies and carrying personnel and light weapons. For Ploughshares purposes, getting to an actual military plane was important.

Mary Kelly's attack on that Navy C-40 had already had some effect on the charter traffic. World Airways, one of the main charter companies hauling troops through Shannon, had decided to stop using the airport. With this first 'result' having been just announced, few of the demonstrators at Shannon that day – they numbered about 300 – were in the mood to condemn Mary Kelly. When the Catholic Worker group joined them, the air of the demonstration was upbeat, though the five were carrying some disappointment about the one that got away.

Their tension was also growing. As Dave parked the car near the demo, gardaí all around, he looked down at Ciaron's feet and saw an assortment of hammers lying there, and even the mattock inevitably sticking out from under the seat. How on earth would they explain all that if a garda happened to look into the car? Angrily he shouted at Ciaron to hide the stuff.

Having missed the AWACS opportunity, the group was not quite ready to settle down at the airport and wait for the next military target. Among other things, the Shannon Peace Camp had been threatened with legal injunctions ordering them off the land by the airport management company, Aer Rianta – though it was not entirely clear that the land in question was Aer Rianta's to seek orders about. Whatever about using a demonstration as a decoy, the five were not inclined to put the camp in further danger. They returned to Glenstal Abbey on the Saturday evening, where Dave told them he had gone with them as far as he could go, and that his driving duties would have to end the following day. The group resolved that the next day they would seek a base closer to the airport with what they hoped would be a sympathetic priest.

The 'rebel priest' is something of a storied figure in the Irish nationalist narrative. While the institutional church was never supportive of 'risings' against British rule – in 1798, 1803, 1848, 1916 etc – there were always individuals who could be counted on to provide spiritual sustenance, at the very least, to Irish rebels. The figure re-emerged during the 'Troubles' of 1968 onwards: while IRA activity in the Republic was low-level, consisting mainly of arms movement and concealment, plus fundraising robberies for the fight in Northern Ireland, the network of political sympathizers in the Southern state inevitably included some priests. This south-west region of Ireland, from Clare through Kerry and

Cork, had been strongly republican in the early 20th century, and the old mix of Catholic piety and nationalism was especially strong here.

Deirdre, Ciaron, Damien, Karen and Nuin, as pacifists, had distinctly mixed attitudes toward late-20th-century Irish republicanism. Irish-Australian Ciaron, the one of them who was drawn from the often deep-green recent diaspora, was also the one most likely to lace his speeches with references to previous forms of Irish anti-imperialist resistance; Deirdre and Damien, having grown up in Ireland through the Troubles, knew just how divisive such language had become. Ciaron, inevitably, could leaven the debate with humour: the Irish, he said, knew all about 'direct action' – it was just *non-violent* direct action they needed a little more help with.

That Sunday, they had a particular 'rebel priest' in mind, who shall remain unnamed here. He was based considerably closer to the airport than Glenstal Abbey, and the five hoped he would let them stay with him, even for a few hours, so they could prepare for an action, then improvise their way the shorter distance to a target. In the Irish tradition what they were looking for would be called a 'safe house'.

On a damp Sunday morning the five left Glenstal, walking down the driveway to avoid the speed bumps, and Dave had a last look around the rooms, checking for lump hammers and the like, and leaving whatever money they could scrape together, along with a thank-you note, in the monastery's wooden box. Their first stop was to attend mass at an old folks' home, where the priest they were looking for was the celebrant. These five diverse but definitely not-elderly people were incongruous at the back of the chapel. They talked to the priest briefly afterwards, and he invited them to his home, the would-be safe-house.

It is not every day, in the secular 21st century, that an Irish priest finds five nice youngish people in his home, eager to talk about theology, peace and justice. He invited them in, cups of tea were made and they settled in for a friendly chat. Damien, the student-priest, began the charm offensive, and the old rebel-priest lent a sympathetic, curious ear to Damien's talk about the importance of praying and the group's rather mysterious need for a place to do it. The fact that Damien had family in the county helped the conversation along, but as far as Ciaron O'Reilly was concerned Moran was going the long way around establishing common ground. Ciaron grew impatient. The nettle would have to be grasped eventually, why not now?

"Listen," Ciaron said. "Let me tell you what we're doing here." And so he did, in a few precisely chosen words.

With a rattle of tea-cups and the color rising to his cheeks the priest got up angrily and literally chased the five out of his house and into the rain.

The five would find no safety within the Church. With some regret they made their way with Dave to the more secular surroundings of the airport and the Shannon Peace Camp. From mid-afternoon on the Sunday they were on foot, their scope limited to the camp, the airport, and the dreary little town of Shannon – which was really little more than a shopping-center parking lot, around which you could get a burger at Supermac's (an Irish variant of you-know-what) or some equally vegetarian-unfriendly pub-grub at the large and fairly charmless local boozer. There was really no question now: they were going to have to act tonight.

They sat in the Shannon pub and finalized their plans, inasmuch as they could amid so much uncertainty about what they would find on the other side of the fence; they finalized too the 'Statement of Faith' they would make to justify the action, and got a press release to Eoin Dubsky for him to release when they confirmed their action by mobile phone. They didn't want to implicate Tom Hyland so after a mobile text message to another friend in Dublin they agreed on the address that Ciaron, Nuin and Karen would give when arrested: 53 Rialto Cottages, in the inner city. Nuin and Karen wrote the address on their arms.

Caoimhe Butterly had arrived in Shannon for the previous day's demo; the five had not seen her since Kildare the previous weekend, and only got a chance to talk to her that Sunday in the pub in Shannon town. Amid some tension and uncertainty, her part in the action, they decided now, would be as 'co-conspirator', a title that, for all its unfortunate Watergate-ish resonances, could possibly put her in some legal jeopardy. Her name (usefully well-known) and biographical details were added to the Statement of Faith. Then, toward evening, the five left her to make final preparations; the tension among them continued however, with Karen and Ciaron arguing – to the point where Karen seriously considered withdrawing from the action.

It was, rather surprisingly, the first time they had stayed at the camp, which at this point consisted of two small mobile-units and six tents of various sorts. The five had no intention of allowing their stay to last over a full night. They hardly interacted with the other campers. They found a wigwam to themselves at the edge of the camp, where they talked and said prayers, commiting themselves to an entirely non-violent action and to peaceful and respectful treatment of anyone they should encounter. There was also a loose sort of ritual involved. Part of the symbolism of many American Plowshares actions involves human blood, often poured on to the military object being damaged. It is, after all, the shedding of blood that the activists are acting to prevent. And moreover, the Christian tradition, and especially the Catholic mass, gives enormous spiritual significance to Jesus Christ's blood – the wine that he transformed, the blood he shed in his Passion and on the cross. The five wanted to honor and show their faith to this tradition. At the same time, the potential evocation of personal martyrdom in spilling their own blood was something the five wanted to avoid: they were not trying to make martyrs of themselves, nor were they engaging in the sort of 'blood sacrifice' that had been such an important (and now widely criticized) part of the Irish past.

So what to do about the blood? They had talked in previous days about finding a doctor who would draw some blood from one of them and then let them have it to use. Even the thought of asking a doctor to do such a thing was off-putting, and the reality never materialized. Maybe in the States, they thought, there are Catholic Worker doctors who take care of this stuff; not in County Clare.

There in the wigwam, they each pricked a finger, drawing a tiny drop of blood. They dripped it into a jar with some water and added to the collection of materials they would take with them.

It was getting to be quite a heavy load – the sort of thing that can happen when you do symbolism by committee. They had some water from St Brigid's Well in Kildare. They had Kathy Kelly's big laminated photos from Iraq. A Bible. A Koran. Rosary beads. Muslim prayer beads. Flowers. Candles. Two apples for 'the goddess'. Two Brigid's Crosses. A couple of videotapes, containing documentaries about Iraq, including John Pilger's *Paying the Price*, which established that war against the Iraqi people had never really stopped.

It was important to get the symbolism right, because with the security at the airport, comparatively symbolic action might be the only sort available to them. Nonetheless, in hope, they also packed the hammers, the mattock, the wire-cutters, spray-paint, flashlight. At the very least they should be able to damage a runway, as Ciaron had done in New York 12 years earlier.

It was about 3am when they left the camp, perhaps 20 minutes later when they reached the fence. From several days' observation Damien Moran knew the basic security routine: a drive-round every 30 minutes outside the perimeter and every 15 minutes inside. They had a window of opportunity. Damien got out the wire-cutters, quickly snipped a hole big enough to get through, and dropped the cutters, never to see them again. Now they were in the big airport grounds, looking for a target, and it was time to crawl. Damien hadn't played hurling at a high level for some time, but he was a fit man and set off across the wet grass beside a taxi runway like something out of (pacifist) boot camp. Nuin and Deirdre were moving in more of a crouching, slightly simian run. Karen was so small she scarcely had to duck down at all.

Ciaron O'Reilly, on the other hand, is a big man, and overnight work in a homeless shelter is not exactly boot-camp preparation, conducive to the highest of fitness levels. He was also fond of a pint of Guinness. Nine months in Ireland had added a few pounds to his frame. And he was carrying a bag full of equipment. Every once in a while the other four would have crawled a few yards out ahead of him across the wet grass, and Ciaron jumped to his feet and ran to catch up, muttering "I'm getting too old for this." No one who saw this scene could easily describe him as 'leader' of this group. Luckily, no one saw this scene.

They moved across the airport's fields and roads for perhaps another quarter-hour. Military craft were not visible on the runway, but Damien had learned enough about the geography of the airport to suspect where one might be stashed – for example, one that was undergoing repairs after being damaged five days earlier by Mary Kelly.

As they neared the SRS hangar most of them stumbled blindly into a drainage ditch. Nuin Dunlop, carrying the huge mattock, had the most dramatic fall, tumbling on to her back while trying to hold the tool up away from her body. For a moment she wasn't sure she would be able to go on. Karen bent over her.

"You take this and go on," Nuin said, handing up the mattock. Karen took the instrument and helped Nuin to her feet. "Come on!"

The hangar was their stopping place. When they got there, the division of labour fell into place: Nuin alone was supposed to concentrate on the shrine, but Karen decided to join her. "Make it on the runway," Ciaron shouted – but there was a big Russian plane parked nearby, so the women, after, they thought, getting a nice wave from a distant Russian, decided to build the shrine right beside the hangar. They dropped to the ground, pulling items from their bags to assemble a shrine, using the photographs Kathy Kelly had given them in Kildare as the center-piece, and the various symbols of Christian and Muslim religious faith and practice. The candles refused to stay lit. Karen and Nuin would have valued the flames even for a little bit of heat.

Deirdre Clancy, with her editorial experience, went to work spray-painting the hangar – most crucially with the words that named it and the airport for what it had become: "Pit Stop of Death" and "Death Port". Then she painted "The War Stops Here" and another RIP for Phil Berrigan. Damien and Ciaron looked for a way into the hangar.

There was a very big door, of course, utterly secured. There was a small wooden-slatted door set in a recess – locked. The latter had glass panels alongside it, but all they could see when they peered through the glass was a small hallway leading to another door. There was a medium-sized metal roller-door, also locked, but as is often the case, the men found there was some give in it, so that it could be raised a couple of inches, with a great effort. With Deirdre's help they held the roller-door up off the ground and looked in turn beneath it, into the brightly lit space on the other side.

Bingo. The plane, Mary Kelly's plane, with its US Navy markings. Ciaron recalled how important the Navy had been in enforcing sanctions and no-fly zones and bombing runs over southern Iraq. Here was the physical embodiment of the murderous war-machine whose consequences could be seen so graphically in Kathy Kelly's photographs. They had to get to this plane and further 'disarm' it – even if it was not an armed aircraft, it was part of the greatest armed apparatus the world has ever known, the US military.

All their strength could not move the roller-door any further. Not even wee Karen Fallon, who anyway was back beside the shrine blowing up her inflatable hammer while Nuin chopped at the runway with the mattock, could have crawled under it, let alone Ciaron O'Reilly. They went back to the small door, with its small glass panels. It was only a question of breaking a glass panel, then, Ciaron thought, perhaps squeezing someone like Karen through the narrow space.

Ciaron ran back to the shrine and grabbed the mattock from Nuin while she was in the middle of a road-gang style swing. He ran again toward the door, the laughing women following him. Both of the side windows were smashed quickly, one by each of the men. Karen was distinctly unimpressed with the idea of scraping her way through a window. Damien looked in through one of them and saw to his relief that the door had an emergency bar for opening it from the inside; reckoning it was an emergency, he reached in, pushed the bar down and pulled the door open. They all went down the hall. Much to their surprise, the door at the other end was unlocked.

It was quarter to four in the morning. Beyond that door was the great high space of the hangar. Garda Sergeant Michael O'Connell, a quiet grey-haired man of a rather sad and nervous disposition, was on duty all alone, in his police uniform and shiny yellow jacket, unarmed like most Irish police. He had been guarding the aircraft, now largely repaired, since 10pm, except for a brief meal break back at Shannon station around 2am, when another cop had covered for him. He had periodically checked all the doors, his footsteps the only sound other than the rumble of the hangar's heating system and the odd shower of rain on the roof.

This was not a space designed for hanging around doing nothing. So for the comfort of the police officers whose job was simply to be there and watch the plane, a Garda car had been parked about 20 feet from its nose. You could sit in there and keep an eye on things, maybe have a little doze…

Sergeant O'Connell got the shock of his life when he looked up and saw five people, from Ciaron O'Reilly with his mattock to Karen Fallon with her balloon – all of them having slipped in quietly and stragglingly – in his hangar, attacking the plane. The C-40 is a modified 737, and sits obligingly low to the ground – baggage handlers hop in and out of a 737's hold without a ladder. The two engines hang from the wings down to just a meter or less from the ground. There was plenty of airplane within easy reach, and after catching breath at the reality of the scene and having a last examination of conscience, each of the five took up a different position. Ciaron had a crack first at the Texas-shaped insignia sported by the 'City of Dallas', while Damien, with the red-handled lump hammer that had been left in the family car all those years ago, hammered the nose of the plane, where there was a radome containing sensitive radar equipment. Deirdre stayed at the near side of the plane, hammering at its fuselage. Nuin and Karen went to the far side and took turns swinging real and inflated hammers, sharing jokes and enjoying the moment.

Sergeant O'Connell radioed for help, shouted at the five, then – perhaps weighing up the options of taking on a dreadlocked giant with a pickaxe, or of struggling with women – he decided he would start his efforts at disarming the disarmers with Damien Moran. He went over and grabbed hold of Damien by the right shoulder, as Damien kept hammering with his left hand, and the grab caused Moran to hit himself in the head with the hammer. Damien the hurler could have shrugged off a tackle like this. But Damien the Ploughshares activist and non-violent witness for peace had a conundrum: he didn't want to stop hammering, but he would not and could not offer any form of resistance that could be regarded as violent. He invited the policeman to join in, and tried to move away from O'Connell, at the same time nearly slipping out of his jacket so that the policeman was clutching at sleeve more than arm. Damien looked with an imploring shrug at Ciaron, seeking philosophical guidance and, well, a little help.

Ciaron put down his mattock and walked over to where this almost-comical struggle was taking place. Years of working with homeless men had thrown up far more difficult situations of coping with aggression and distress than this one. Ciaron laid his hand on Sergeant O'Connell's back and gently rubbed it, explaining why the five were there, explaining that they meant no harm to anyone, that he could join them if he liked but at any rate shouldn't worry. The sergeant said, repeatedly, he was afraid of losing his job. The men made it clear that they would submit to arrest when they had completed their action. (As Dan Berrigan implores: "Don't just do something, stand there.") By this time Damien was completely out of his jacket, and Sergeant O'Connell dropped it to the ground.

The five went back to disarming the plane. Ciaron went to the nose-cone and swung the mattock repeatedly, punching large holes in the thin metal skin of the craft. With a lot of damage done, police reinforcements imminent and especially with Sergeant O'Connell in a distressed state, most of them thought it was time to stop. Deirdre made a quick phonecall to report on the action so that the prepared press release could be issued, with the news that they had reached and damaged a plane, then she got on her knees to pray at the front of the plane. Damien, Nuin and Karen joined in. O'Reilly wasn't so sure, and shouted for help to move a ladder around so he, or perhaps Karen, could get up and break the cockpit windows. But the consensus was that they should lay down their tools: O'Reilly joined the other four and sat in a circle near the front of the plane. They sang the song they had heard Luka Bloom play two days earlier, 'I Am Not at War with Anyone', then Damien led them through the Rosary. They passed the objects they had used out of the circle and laid them on the ground beside them. Karen noticed an open crate nearby, and inside it the nosecone that Mary Kelly had damaged the previous week.

Moments later, Denis Swift and Noel McNulty were the first gardaí to arrive at the scene as O'Connell's back-up, with airport police close behind. They witnessed an extraordinary scene: five people praying on the floor, their tools beside them, a plane punched with dents and holes, and their colleague in a state of considerable anxiety. After names were taken and Ciaron was handcuffed as he sat on the floor, Garda Swift followed the route through which the five had entered the building, finding the broken window and, not far from there, the shrine. He noted the contents for his report: "harrowing pictures of children; candle holders, candles, a copy of the bible, a copy of the Koran, a lump hammer, 2 apples, about 4 bouquets of flowers and 2 Saint Bridget crosses." Never thinking either of this shrine's sanctity, nor of its relevance as evidence in this 'assembled' form, Swift threw the shrine's contents into the rucksack that was on the ground beside it, and tossed them all into the patrol car.

It was about 4.30am by the time the five had been quizzed about their ownership of the various tools on the floor – they answered cooperatively – and they were driven by Swift and the airport police to Shannon Garda Station. In the west of Ireland in early February, it was still the dead and dark of night, but it was sure to be only the beginning of a long and grueling day for the Pitstop Ploughshares – the name they adopted for their action and, by extension, themselves. Eoin Dubsky sent out their press release, with their successful attack on the plane buried beneath the account of the symbolic actions that were, in effect, the back-up plan if they had not reached a significant target. Apart from basically missing the story, however, it was a good statement, complete with weblinks, addresses, media references and brief pen-portraits of the group, including co-conspirator Caoimhe Butterly. It read, in part:

> In the early hours of Monday 03 February, five members of the pacifist Catholic Worker movement cut their way into Shannon Airport (see http://www.refuelingpeace.org/). The peace activists poured human blood on the runway that has been servicing US military flights, troop and munition deployments to US military bases in Kuwait and Qatar. They constructed a shrine on the runway to Iraqi children killed and threatened by US/British bombardment and sanctions. The shrine consisted of copies of the Bible and Quran, rosary and muslim prayer beads, flowers, photographs of Iraqi children and Brigid's crosses. They then began to take up the runway, working on its edge with a mallet. [sic]
>
> The activists approached the hangar housing the US Navy plane under repair. They painted "Pit stop of death" on the hangar's roller door, and began the dismantling of the hangar. Others entered the hangar to disarm the repaired US warplane.
>
> The five activists were arrested by gardaí. They refuse to co-operate with bail conditions, have initiated a fast for peace and a call for mass nonviolent resistance to Irish complicity in the forthcoming war on Iraq. They are likely to be moved to Limerick Prison. The acts of witness will continue in and out of prison.

The Catholic Worker movement, founded by Dorothy Day in New York City in 1933, consists of small faith-based communities serving the homeless and nonviolently resisting war preparations (see http://www.catholicworker.org/).

Ploughshares acts of nonviolent disarmament were initiated by radical priests Fr Philip and Daniel Berrigan in the US in the 1980s. These nonviolent actions have addressed nuclear and conventional weapon systems by enfleshing the prophesy of Isaiah Ch. 2. Some activists have been acquitted of all charges, others have received prison sentences of up to 18 years. (See http://www.plowsharesactions.org/)

It proceeded with a 'Statement of Faith' from the five, and Caoimhe, that set out the rationale for the action:

We come to Shannon Airport to carry out an act of life-affirming disarmament in a place of preparations for slaughter.

Like the railway tracks that ran to the town of Auschwitz, the runway at Shannon has been militarized for service on an assembly line of death. The train tracks at Auschwitz brought people to their deaths, the runway at Shannon brings death to the people. The Irish Government acts in contravention of the Irish Constitution, International Law and divine mandate to service US military aircraft, troop and munition deployments.

The U.S./British war on the Iraqi people, and for Iraqi resources, has been long and varied. The U.S./U.K. military has claimed over 2 million Iraqi lives

· in their financial and military support for the Saddam Hussein regime in the '70s and '80s

· in their hi tech bombing campaign of 1991

· in the 12 years of crippling sanctions imposed on the Iraqi people

· and now their plans to conquer and occupy Iraq

U.S./U.K. weapons manufacturers also continue to fuel the daily grind of death and destruction inflicted on the Palestinian people.

SWORDS INTO PLOUGHSHARES

We come to Shannon Airport around the Feast of St. Brigid, to disarm and disable the war machine. We hope to begin to take up the runway and ground military aircraft. We hope to be joined in this act of disarmament by those who encounter us. Citizens, police and soldiers wielding hammers brought down the Berlin Wall; we hope all will pitch in to take up this runway and ground planes servicing the war machine. We find this easier to envision than the further slaughter of Iraqi children that U.S. British and Irish governments wish us to consider.

We act inspired by Brigid and Irish traditions of healing and peacemaking. We carry out Christ's commandment to "love our enemies" by nonviolently resisting the slaughter of their children. We attempt to enflesh the prophesy of Isaiah Ch 2 and Micah Ch 4 "to beat swords into ploughshares".

We respond to the call of the prophets of Modern America. Catholic Worker founder Dorothy Day, who encourages us "to fill the jails with nonviolent resistance to war"; Martin Luther King, who warns us that we are confronted by "a choice between nonviolence and nonexistence". Fr Daniel Berrigan, who observes: "We have assumed the name of peacemakers, but we have been, by and large, unwilling to pay any significant price. And because we want peace with half a heart and half a life and will, the war, of course continues, because the waging of war, by its nature is total – but the waging of peace, by our cowardice is partial."

Chapter 5

Inside and Out

NEEDLESS TO SAY, THIS DEEPLY FELT STATEMENT DIDN'T stand a chance in the mainstream media against the spinning that came from the authorities. A germ of truth – that Sergeant O'Connell had been distressed by the action – metastasized into a series of lies that characterized the five, and their action, as violent. The key word in the official narrative was "overpowered": the accused, according to the police account, "overpowered the garda on duty". 'Overwhelmed' might have been a better word – but "overpowered", which sounded like assault, had a pernicious influence on how the case was reported and discussed in the first days after the action.

That morning Associated Press report, wired around the world, was typical. Littered with errors, it began:

> Police arrested five anti-war activists Monday on suspicion of overpowering a guard and attacking a US Navy plane with axes and hammers, the second such assault against American military flights through this officially neutral nation.

Cathy O'Halloran, the regional news correspondent for the Irish national broadcaster, RTE, made the speculative most of the O-word. Her report that morning stated: "They overpowered a garda who was on duty and did further damage to a US Navy plane... They'll probably face charges of criminal damage, but could face much more serious charges arising out of overpowering the garda on duty." The Minister for Transport, Seamus Brennan – whose TV promise of no more incidents had been exposed as political folly – chimed in angrily: "The blame here has to be quite squarely laid with the section of peace protesters who went and challenged a garda – the garda ended up in hospital, doin' his duty... The people who have questions to answer are the small minority of 'peaceful protesters' who attack the police force, the gardaí, of our own state." Taoiseach Bertie Ahern joined the chorus: "I think now we see that maybe we've been a bit over-tolerant with peaceful protesters when they're not one bit peaceful." The police press spokesman told a version of the story whereby, despite being initially "overpowered", the cop on duty had kept damage to a minimum.

The claim and implication of violence was completely untrue, as was the suggestion that Sergeant O'Connell had substantially disrupted the incident in any way other than by attracting the pity and concern of the accused. But some of this spin could charitably be ascribed to confusion rather than malice. When the senior officer from Shannon, Superintendent John Kerins, arrived at the hangar at 4.50am, after the accused had gone, he found Sergeant O'Connell shaking and pale. Kerins advised the sergeant to go to a doctor or hospital to get checked out – this advice, or rather some further mention of it, must have been the origin of the erroneous story of 'hospitalization.' O'Connell, by his own account, saw a doctor at the station in the early hours of the morning, then, after going off-duty, he visited his own doctor, who gave him medication to ease his trauma and distress.

Indeed, it seems from the transcripts of the initial police questioning of the arrested people that officers were concerned about some harm having been done to their colleague. At about 9am, Detective Sergeant Joe O'Brien asked Deirdre Clancy: "Did you assault a garda who was on duty at the airport hangar?" She answered, as she did to nearly all the questions: "No comment." A few minutes later he tried again: "There was a member of the Garda Síochána terrorized this morning, how do you feel about that?" This question seemed to confuse Deirdre, who seemed unsure it referred to anything that had happened in the hangar, replying:

"I have nothing to say about that because it was something that I did not witness."

Doubts seemed to creep in among the police, because after 10:30am O'Brien was using the word "intimidated" to describe what had allegedly happened to Sergeant O'Connell. By the time Karen Fallon was interviewed at lunchtime no mention was made at all of any problems relating to O'Connell, who had gone from "assaulted" to "terrorized" to "intimidated" over the course of two hours. "Comforted" was, you might think, a verb too far.

But in fact it wasn't. By noon, as Damien Moran was being questioned, he was actually asked: "Did you comfort a member of the gardaí?... Have no comment on the fact that a member of the gardaí was seriously traumatized by your actions?... Would it concern you that a member has been traumatized?" To this last question Damien, otherwise sticking manfully to stare-at-the-wall interview tactics, could not resist answering, "Yes."

A couple of the questioners moved the focus, concentrating on the trauma to the local economy. One asked Karen: "Do you realize that people are going to lose their jobs in Shannon over the actions of you and others this morning?"

Karen and Nuin were both caught reading their alleged address from the numbers and letters scrawled on their upper arms. A police interrogator was understandably skeptical and asked Nuin: "53 Rialto Cottages is not your address, is it?... Do you know the postcode for that address?"

Nuin gave her standard reply: "I don't wish to comment on that right now."

It is hard to tell what precisely the cops asking the questions thought they were going to find out in these interviews, in which they drift from philosophical questions to ones drawn from gangland drama. "Are you part of this group or do you work freelance?" one asked Karen.

Ciaron understatingly told his early-morning interviewer: "I am not convinced that the process we are having is a genuine search for truth. What you are doing is a systematic cover-up of the deaths of one and a half million children and the serious constitutional obligation you have taken as gardaí to defend the Constitution. It obliges you to investigate how that Constitution is being undermined…. Until I am convinced you are investigating the issue seriously, I can't accept more questions." When the questions inevitably continued, he repeated the point: "This dialogue is not an authentic search for the truth, therefore I wish to exercise my legal right not to answer any more questions. That was very much Jesus's response when questioned by authorities in similar circumstances."

Suspects citing Jesus and calling themselves 'Catholic' must have been disorientating for police in a country where that word means little more than attending mass on Sunday and doing what you are told. One garda put the question succinctly if rather strangely to Damien: "If you are a Catholic do you believe that what you did this morning is correct?" Getting no reply, he moved to find other words to identify Damien's governing philosophy: "Are you anti-America?... Are you anti-British?... Are you anti-authority?"

Amidst the inanity of most of the questioning, there were some significant answers. At lunchtime, Damien broke his string of "no comments" to answer the question, "Do you know why you have been arrested?"

His response was: "Criminal damage but I believe it was disarmament."

At 3pm, Damien got even more specific, asking to be interviewed so that he could give a one-line statement: "I honestly believe I had a lawful excuse to commit an act of disarmament to protect the lives and property of myself and others."

Damien Moran's close paraphrase of the wording of a defence available under the criminal-damage statute should have come as no surprise to anyone who had closely followed Eoin Dubsky's legal tactics in his own spray-painting case. Unfortunately few people, even in the anti-war movement, had paid close attention, and Damien's salient summary was confined to the case file at Shannon rather than put into the public domain. The idea that the Pitstop Ploughshares action could have legal as well as moral justification simply didn't occur to most people. An editorial in the *Irish Times*, normally the dull embodiment of caution, was precipitous and premature enough to call the arrested activists "law-breakers."

Even the moral argument was getting short shrift. The Green Party was the major political organization most closely associated with the anti-war movement, but its leader Trevor Sargent was cornered into condemning the Shannon action while the "overpowered" spin was in the ascendancy. However, after the garda-assault story had been discredited, the party chairman John Gormley – after criticizing the irresponsible and erroneous coverage of the action – said it was "vital that the protesters do not continue to play into the hands of the warmongers and their allies." His party, he said, wanted "protest to adhere strictly to a passive resistance code. We cannot afford to lose the battle for the hearts and minds of ordinary people."

The NGO Peace Alliance, to which some religious-based organizations were affiliated, also quickly went on the attack. Within hours of the action, its spokesman Brendan Butler called it "counter-productive" and insisted on the use of "peaceful means only," apparently taking it as given that the Pitstop Ploughshares had utilized some other, non-peaceful means. The NGO Peace Alliance had joined forces with the Irish Anti-War Movement and the small Peace and Neutrality Alliance to organize the "international day of protest" coming up on February 15th. They had been remarkably successful in attracting favorable media attention and had reason to believe it could be a big demonstration, perhaps numbering in the tens of thousands. Like Gormley, Butler was thinking of the delicate "ordinary people": events like the one at Shannon, he said, "only frightened supporters of this peaceful action."

Within 48 hours of the action, the Shannon Peace Camp had decided to disband. The airport operating company, Aer Rianta, was close to securing a High Court injunction against a few dozen named people, banning them from airport property. But at least some of the campers were prepared to cite the Mary Kelly and Pitstop Ploughshares actions as their reason for leaving, saying not only that many people did not support such "vandalism," but that a media circus had been created, which detracted from the real issues at the airport. Mary Kelly was just deciding to accept bail, under conditions which included staying out of County Clare, but her 13-year-old daughter Julie, another camper, was not happy to see the camp disbanded or actions like her mother's blamed. Even she admitted, however, that with the Irish Army coming in to protect the airport's seven-mile perimeter, the scene at Shannon was getting difficult.

Meanwhile the Pitstop Ploughshares had a long and complicated first day or two in custody, with the defendants being dragged through interviews, and in a police van to a remote Clare town for a sitting of the District Court. They were each charged with two counts of criminal damage, one for the hangar windows and one for the US aircraft itself.

Would there be any possibility of bail in this case – for a set of defendants charged with simple damage to property, and with no previous arrest record in the jurisdiction? Amid an atmosphere of hysteria in the media and in the courtroom, the impressively massive Garda Inspector Tom Kennedy told Ennis District Court rather cogently and accurately: "On the basis of the information given to the court, these people see it as their right and duty to interfere with aircraft landing at Shannon."

Their lawyer, solicitor Joe Noonan, was more eloquent, however. He denied and denounced the media suggestion that his clients had engaged in any violence against anyone, noting the absence of any assault charge against them. Here, he said, were defendants who were entirely peaceful and acknowledging of what they had done, prepared to account for their actions and as people of honour give their word that they would appear for trial. These accused would be doubly bound if they were released on bail, he said. After all, the very essence of their defence put their character at issue. If they gave their word that they would turn up for trial and then broke it, it would torpedo their defence as people of exceptional moral character.

Noonan's argument carried less weight with the judge than the policeman's. The five were remanded in custody to Limerick Prison, a half-hour's drive from the airport.

As they 'checked in' to Limerick late on the Monday evening, part of the routine paperwork was to ask each of them for a religious affiliation. Karen Fallon, who earlier in the day had repeatedly asked her interrogators for a chance to get some sleep, had enough energy and spirit to offer the jailers a small discourse on her various pagan and wicca influences. Ciaron remembered that Catholic masses in the jail might give the Catholic Worker group a chance to meet together, and gave Karen a metaphorical elbow in the ribs, muttering under his breath: "Catholic, Catholic."

"Right, Catholic," Karen agreed. As it turned out, however, men and women had separate masses in the prison. Nevertheless, the five quickly found that they could meet together when they had visitors, or to receive spiritual guidance from one of the brothers who would drive down from Glenstal Abbey.

Ciaron and Damien shared a cell in the men's section, while Deirdre, Nuin and Karen were together in the women's. The five were still getting to know each other, and prison offered plenty of time to bond. As remand prisoners they had a relatively relaxed visiting regime, and they were touched by the support of some friends. Tim Hourigan was broke at the time, but he would hitchhike several times a week from the 'peace house' flat in Shannon so he could meet with the five in jail, sharing his warmth and his latest planespotting results.

It was just as well that the Ploughshares tradition, especially its US variant, placed such a high value on this sort of jail time. When the state authorities did agree to set some bail conditions in that first week, they were absolutely intolerable to anyone who was not thoroughly desperate to be free. Ciaron O'Reilly and Karen Fallon continued to be denied bail entirely, and the conditions offered to the other three included a personal surety of 3,000 euros each; twice-daily appearances at a designated Garda station; staying out of County Clare (which happens to be one of Ireland's largest); agreeing not to confer with each other before their trial or trials; and staying at least one mile clear of the US embassy in Dublin. These restrictions, especially the one on conferring and the one that would tie each of them to a particular Garda station, no doubt far from Shannon, were extraordinary limits on their freedom by any measure. Remanded defendants accused of rape or murder would generally sign on with the police no more than two or three times a week; Mary Kelly was expected to appear three times a week at a station in west County Cork. Twice-daily would mean they could scarcely budge.

Deirdre, Damien and Nuin refused the conditions, both for themselves and in solidarity with Ciaron and Karen. The five could sit tight for a while, and Ciaron – always an articulate and loquacious writer, as Indymedia readers could testify – used the opportunity to write an upbeat letter, which went up on that website on February 10th, a week after the action. It began "Dear Friends", and was clearly an effort to make friends, to introduce and explain the Catholic Worker group and its traditions to a largely ignorant Irish anti-war community.

> Shannon has become a major pitstop for U.S troop and munition movement into Kuwait and Qatar. The witness [i.e. the action] once again reveals the twin reality that the weapons are not secure! / the weapons don't secure us! Over 90 Ploughshares communities over the last 23 years all arrived at the weapon systems they hope to disarm – many located in more intense security environments than the hangar at Shannon. The presence of US troops and munitions in Ireland en route to war is not only unconstitutional but endangers Iraqi, Irish and American lives.

The action itself was beautiful. After crawling through the sludge and muck of the airfield in the early hours of Feb 4th [sic, it was the 3rd], we arrived at the hangar. The repairs on the warplane from Mary Kelly's disarmament action the previous week had just been completed hours before. We spray-painted the hangar... We constructed a shrine with photos of Iraqi children (joyous suffering under sanctions, killed by bombing), copies of the Bible and Quran, Islamic and rosary beads, St Brigid's crosses, flowers. Human blood and water from Brigid's well was poured on the runway and a mattock was used to begin to take the runway up. On the mattock was inscribed the Dorothy Day quote: "IF THEY SHOULD COME FOR THE INNOCENT WITHOUT STEPPING OVER YOUR BODY, CURSED BE YOUR RELIGION AND YOUR LIFE!"

We managed to access the hangar making our way into the main area containing the U.S navy war plane. We began to disarm the plane....

A garda was parked in the hangar. He pretty much suffered a panic attack during the disarmament. We tried to reassure and comfort him during the disarmament. I guess those on guard at the tomb went through similar emotions during the resurrection. The only fears expressed by the garda was of the response of the authorities (e.g. he may lose his job!), he expressed no fear of us. After disabling the plane, we knelt around our inflatable hammer, reciting the rosary and singing.

The state reaction to our witness has been an avalanche of lies, slander and hysteria.... The government then deployed the army (150 soldiers and 4 armoured personnel carriers).... WORLD AIRWAYS announced it was rerouting its flights through Frankfurt and we are generally being blamed for single handedly collapsing the economy in South West Ireland! Aer Rianta tried serving a high court injunction on us in the prison.

Upon arrest we began a fast in solidarity with the people of Iraq suffering under sanctions. Court support has been good, with friends travelling from Cork, Galway, Dublin, Essex, Limerick, Shannon Peace camp and house, to express solidarity. It has been great to have Nuria [Mustafa] from Iraq and her daughter in court with us. Very moving when she offered her home as a bail address for Nuin, the U.S citizen in our group. From the people of Iraq to the people of the U.S to the people of Iraq – gifts of nonviolent resistance, hospitality and solidarity! We broke our fast together on the 5th day after the action.

We are a community drawn from the Irish experience. Deirdre is from Dublin, Damien from the midlands. Karen, Nuin and I spring from the Irish diaspora. We come from Irish communities in 3 nations that have been involved in this genocidal war of sanctions and bombing against the people of Iraq – Britain, US and Australia. We are a very young community. Karen and I have known each other for a few years through the Nipponzan Myōhōji Buddhist Temple in Milton Keynes, the London Catholic Worker squat and the Faslane Peace Camp in Scotland where she had lived for the last couple of years. I met Deirdre at the end of October, Damien in November, Nuin on New Year's Day. The community building and witness have been rushed due to the impending war that will disrupt and destroy many lives. We really need your love and solidarity to grow and stand steadfast as a community, to fully explore the ploughshares prophecy unleashed.

We have managed to piss off some extremely powerful people and the word has come down the line to hang us out to dry. This was evident at the recent bail hearing where Karen and I were denied bail outright and restrictive conditions to gag us were imposed on Damien, Deirdre and Nuin.

We remain in Limerick prison in solidarity with all those in the firing line of this genocidal war machine and all those on the loose and in chains nonviolently resisting it.

Love and Solidarity,
Ciaron O'Reilly.

PS Inflatable hammers are a welcome symbol of visual solidarity with us. They're available from tourist shops on O'Connell Street, Dublin.

It cannot be said this eloquent message made much of an impact in the outside world. The Irish media had got over its few days of irresponsibly speculative coverage of the story, culminating in University

College Dublin law lecturer Tom Cooney going on TV, unopposed, to explain that the five could not possibly have any legal defence for their action, and the *Ireland on Sunday* tabloid's farrago of nonsense under the headline "Runway Voodoo", painting the five as a weirdo cult. By the time O'Reilly's letter was made public, the media had moved into its more normal *sub judice* mode, in which any matter that is before the courts, at whatever stage, is regarded as untouchable, lest coverage might be prejudicial. (The freewheeling US crime and court coverage is regarded in Ireland with a mix of horror and envy.) So, even leaving aside the press's usual political prejudices, there was no chance that "the action was beautiful" was going to be picked up by the main newspapers. Even on Indymedia, the inevitable arguments about where war-resisters should draw the line revealed an Irish Left that was remarkably ignorant of, and hostile to, ideas about civil disobedience and non-violent direct action that would be commonplace in other dissident cultures. Sinn Fein, which had for decades defended the political violence of the IRA, could not bring itself to speak up in favor of Mary Kelly and the Pitstop Ploughshares. Across the Left the concern about alienating 'ordinary people' was voiced, in anticipation of the February 15th demonstration. The media had been remarkably supportive of well-mannered anti-war discussion and was full of plugs for the demo – not to quite the same extent as in Britain, where two or three national daily newspapers transformed their front-pages into virtual poster sites, but enough that activists were tempted to temper their message to keep RTE and most of the papers onside.

O'Reilly's final plea for inflatable hammer-carrying, like his plug for an O'Connell Street shop, was clearly aimed at people planning to march in that demonstration through the centre of Dublin. However, when that bright Saturday afternoon finally arrived, there were few hammer-bearers to be found. Instead, there was perhaps the most extraordinary political gathering seen in Ireland since Daniel O'Connell's 'monster meetings' of the early 19th century. It seemed that along with the usual suspects, all of respectable liberal Dublin had turned out, a first political outing for many since the days when anti-apartheid marches could bring forth tens of thousands of people in support of freedom in faraway South Africa. Amid the printed signs being distributed by the Socialist Workers Party and other far-left groups were thousands of handwritten ones, being carried by everyone from toddlers to grannies. Many of them predictably bashed Bush and called, in naive hope, for more UN negotiations to avert war in Iraq, but plenty more displayed how well 'ordinary people' understood the petroleum basis for the impending war, and how angry they felt about the government's shenanigans over Shannon in support of that war.

The march organizers were blessed not merely with a huge crowd, but with RTE News assigning its most excitable correspondent, Charlie Bird, to lead the coverage from the streets. Thus viewers of the 6pm TV news broadcast, including thousands of marchers who had repaired to pubs all over the city, saw Charlie shouting at them that perhaps as many as 150,000 people had snaked their way around the city centre. Even most optimistically-minded activists were surprised at that huge number, but it stuck in the public's mind, and any attempt by the police to impose their typical low estimates wouldn't stand a chance against the rather odd authority of Charlie Bird. Thus February 15th, 2003, in Dublin must stand as one of the very few occasions on which the standard and accepted media count of a left-oriented political demonstration may have actually been an overestimate.

That is in itself a measure of how benignly much of Official Ireland looked at the demo. Taoiseach (prime minister) Bertie Ahern, with typical slipperiness, declared himself pleased at the turnout, because he too was opposed to war. Inasmuch as the demo had attacked his posture on Shannon, well of course, he said, the use of the airport would be reviewed in the event of an actual invasion of Iraq, but that hadn't happened yet.

The benign response to the march may have had another dimension too: the organizers, who had rounded up an impressive array of political speakers, kept the disarmament actions at Shannon strictly off the stage – or rather stages, because there were three separate points for speeches along the march route. Eoin Dubsky and Mary Kelly were not among the many people making speeches. The Pitstop Ploughshares, still in jail in Limerick for their brave and risky action, did not get a single mention from the platforms.

Ciaron O'Reilly was faced with clear evidence that his effort to make friends had fallen on deaf ears. He shot off another prison letter, which went on to Indymedia on the following Tuesday, February 18th. He started off with praise for the size and pluralism of the London and Dublin marches, but noted that the US "had not missed a war-drum beat." Then he really turned the screw, with an outburst that could have been modeled on Jesus among the money-changers:

> If truth be told, what put the issue of Irish complicity in this US war on the front burner was largely a number of solo efforts (Tim [Hourigan]'s planespotting, Eoin [Dubsky]'s one man/ one spray can/ one barrister engagement of a Hercules and an Irish High Court, Mary's spontaneous disarmament of a US navy plane) and a couple of fragile collective efforts (the 4-week Shannon Peace Camp and us the "Pit Stop Ploughshares" lightning striking twice on the very same/ recently repaired/ security guaranteed US navy plane). This is not to ignore the grassroots education and rallying work by SWP/ IAWM/ Grassroots Network/ WSM [the anarchist Workers Solidarity Movement]/ local peace groups – but it was really these acts of direct nonviolent resistance that took the game to the government.
>
> Surprise, surprise – none of these resisters were allowed to address the crowd at Saturday's rally in Dublin. The speakers' platform was grid locked by opportunists, careerists, church and political bureaucrats desperately attempting to lead/hijack the movement. We have created the space for these bureaucrats to operate, colonize the space and sell us out. The scripture (John 10:12) refers

to these folks as the "Hirelings": their job is to control and manage dissent – channel it, contain it and kill it on behalf of the wolf.

The demonisation of our Ploughshares community by the state and attempted marginalisation of imprisoned resisters by the movement bureaucrats is a result of us breaking a "gentleman's agreement" between the state and these "legitimate voices of dissent". The Irish state decrees that "you can have your protests as long as we can have our war!" When we disarmed the US navy plane at Shannon we moved from protest to resistance, breaking this agreement. The response (as predicted in Mark 13:9) was arrest, criminalisation, prison, lies, slander, troop deployment, Aer Rianta civil injunction, denunciation of friends, warm friends cooling and apparently censorship from the platform at Saturday's Dublin peace rally.

This isn't a whinge, it's a political analysis of the dynamics between the state-radicals-moderates/liberal – just the way it is/has always been, acknowledge it, shed false expectations of solidarity from such quarters, celebrate the solidarity flowing our way form decent folks who see the war as something to resist rather than some kind of marketing opportunity – and move on! Move on to what? Solidarity and resistance!

We must not be seduced into slumber by the self-congratulatory rhetoric of those who wish to contain our movement – with non-violent resistance the movement must always maintain the initiative....

It was a far cry from the "Dear Friends" and "Love and Solidarity" of a mere week earlier, though Ciaron did end it with a rallying call for a March 1st protest at Shannon, when the anarchist-based Grassroots Network was planning a mass trespass. Even with that there was no mistaking Ciaron's message: as far as he was concerned, the 'mainstream' of the anti-war movement had made clear its feelings about the likes of the Pitstop Ploughshares; now Ciaron, at whatever political risk, was returning the compliment.

Chapter 6

Watch and Wait

MARCH 1st PROVED TO BE A FATEFUL, NOT TO SAY FARCICAL, day for the Irish anti-war community and its campaign on Shannon Airport, and nearly a dangerous one for Ciaron O'Reilly.

On the wider front, the Irish Anti-War Movement had decided to call a 'mass demonstration' at Shannon on Saturday, March 1st, not to be confused with the previously planned Grassroots Network 'mass trespass' on the same day. But confused, of course, it was. Divisions emerged in anti-war ranks, and the media – tired already of all the benign toddlers and grannies of February 15th fame – seized on the arguments with delight. Respectable and mainstream political-party support fell away from the IAWM demo, as those who had basked in the glory of the Dublin success feared being associated with a scene that might just turn ugly. The IAWM's leadership core, much of it from the Socialist Workers Party, must have resented such blatant displays of fair-weather friendship, but its bitterness was turned less on the popular friends it still hoped to regain than on the hippie/anarchist fringe that was causing all the difficulty with this trespass talk.

In the end, two separate demonstrations occurred, starting at different times, and neither group came out of the day very well. A high-spirited few hundred Grassrooters discovered that announcing a trespass weeks in advance makes such a thing very difficult to accomplish, against serried ranks of well-fortified police, and it duly wasn't. The IAWM march was probably a bit bigger, but its ranks felt demoralizingly diminished after the Dublin hoards of a fortnight earlier; and the yellow-jacketed march stewards warning people to stay away from the nasty anarchist Grassroots crowd just down the road looked absurd, sectarian and more than a little anal. Any 'neutrals' who turned up on the day must have felt bewildered and put-off. The scent of political danger and failure around protest at Shannon that had started with the Mary Kelly and Pitstop Ploughshares action, and turned stronger with the hasty dismantling of the Shannon Peace Camp, now seemed to be a stench. (Whether it was a phantom odour is another question: three charter companies carrying troops actually pulled out of Shannon in February after the two actions, when Shannon looked like it could be more trouble than it was worth. They were coming back now when it was getting obvious that the airport was more secure and the campaign was faltering. Little else happened at Shannon apart from a Good Friday action in March when two activists planted potatoes along the runway.)

Ciaron O'Reilly, meanwhile, had spent much of February wondering if the Pitstop Ploughshares might make more friends – including among the more tactically amenable but politically suspicious Grassroots grouping, where a friendly embrace of a group labelled 'Catholic' was problematic – if at least some of the defendants were out of jail advocating their position. He also had an offer to start regular work at the 'wet shelter' for homeless men in Dublin at the beginning of March. The five's trusted solicitor Joe Noonan had introduced them to a barrister, a dedicated lawyer named Giollaiosa Ó Lideadha, who's uncommon first name means 'Servant of Jesus' and who had been organizing a 'Lawyers Against War' group and was keenly interested in fighting the case. In the latest hearings, an offer of bail had been extended to Karen and Ciaron, and the conditions attached had been relaxed a little: they would have to sign on with the cops 'only' once a day and, crucially, they would be allowed to confer with each other before trial – Ciaron expected that in fact they would live in community as the Dublin Catholic Worker. Thus, somewhat to his own surprise, Ciaron allowed himself to be first out of jail, on Friday, February 28th.

Dave Donnellan collected him that afternoon. Ciaron was definitely 'on for a pint' to mark his freedom, so they planned a trip to the pub, with Ciaron planning to catch the last train to Dublin and Dave staying in Limerick to visit the remaining prisoners and attend a Shannon demo. Irish pubs, however, have a way of disrupting plans, and Ciaron missed his train. He and Dave booked into a B&B near the train station.

The new plan was for Ciaron to hang around Limerick for the Saturday, maybe getting a chance to wave at busloads of demonstrators as they rode through town to Shannon – where he was banned by his bail conditions. That morning Dave was the first one down to breakfast, and as he sat at the window supping his morning tea, he noticed a Garda van parked outside the establishment, and a policeman getting out of it. Dave didn't think much of it. There were a lot of police around Limerick in advance of that day's dual (duel?) demonstrations down the road at the airport. After breakfast, and in no great hurry to get back to Dublin on a Saturday morning, they got newspapers so they could read up on the latest rows over Shannon, the self-destruction of the Irish anti-war campaign and news of the war that hadn't even started yet. Ciaron was also, as always, keen to keep track of Manchester United's fortunes. They were on their beds perusing the pages when a knock came on the door.

"Yeah," Ciaron said. The door opened on two of the plainsclothes cops always known in Ireland as "Special Branch men". One entered and Ciaron jumped up to face him. "Are you Ciaron O'Reilly?" Dave stayed on his bed peering over the paper.

Ciaron resisted the temptation to tell them that he was the *other* giant dreadlocked Australian sporting anti-war gear and known to have been in the Limerick area. Instead he refused to answer and asked to see their IDs. They went off and presumably got enough further information on the man they were seeking to ensure that they had found none other than Ciaron O'Reilly. They returned a few minutes later, and told him as much, adding that he was breaking his bail conditions, since he should have signed on in a Dublin Garda station already. Ciaron was blocking the door at this point and demanding that they display a search warrant for the room – though the cops had expressed no particular interest in searching the room at all. They went off with no clear indication of what they would do next.

Dave was struck not just by the strangeness of the exchange, and by the danger that Ciaron was going to be thrown back in jail just a day after his release on bail, but by the extreme, almost mild-mannered politeness of the Special Branch men. They seemed to address Ciaron with something definitely resembling respect. They certainly didn't seem anxious to arrest him. Ciaron wasn't sure if the cops were bluffing about his bail, so he phoned Joe Noonan to see if he really shouldn't have stayed so long in Limerick. Noonan confirmed that he was probably in breach of his bail conditions and needed to be careful about his signing-on in future. Dave and Ciaron left the B&B shortly after – though not before the latter got a chance to throw a few choice words at the proprietor, who he suspected of ratting on him to the police.

As Ciaron got down to the difficult work of advocacy in the outside world, the rest of the group emerged from prison only gradually. Deirdre and Nuin paid their bail and left in early March. Nuin got a variation in her bail conditions: she wouldn't have to stay a mile away from the US embassy, since she was, after all, a US citizen, however unlikely to be seeking consular services. Deirdre too successfully argued that for a freelance editor to be forced to stay clear of a large swathe of southeast Dublin would be an unreasonable restriction on her working capacity. Damien, however, would not be allowed to visit his relations in County Clare.

Damien lasted about a fortnight in prison after his roommate left, in the meantime (with typical enthusiasm) teaching geography and mathematics to his fellow prisoners, and setting up a prayer-and-study group, Lexio Divinio, in which he was joined by a guy who was in for manslaughter, another who was a convicted pedophile and a third who was a heroin addict. Damien got a letter from a neighbour back in Banagher telling him how he was breaking his mother's heart. His mother didn't visit him, confiding in a friend that if she were let near her son the authorities would have to find room in the prison for her – because she was sure to try to kill him.

When Damien did leave Limerick, he fully expected trouble back in Kimmage – and half-hoped that he would be kicked out of the seminary to spare him having to choose among the three options that seemed available to him: an open life with Dorota, a priestly life without her, or the priesthood with a secret lover. (His own philosophical objections to imposed celibacy were strong enough to make him feel capable of the apparent hypocrisy of the last option.) The Holy Ghost fathers, however, didn't make life so easy for him, accepting him warmly back into the seminary.

Even when he decided soon after, in the comfort of Kimmage, that he would abandon his studies for the priesthood, the fathers said Damien could continue to live at the seminary, and they even allowed Ciaron to come join him there.

Karen Fallon, realising she was going to be confined to Ireland on her release and with little there to come out to, was the last left inside. She wrote defiantly from prison in mid-March, as the countdown to war resounded with unquestionable inevitability:

> The Dublin Catholic Worker ploughshares action at Shannon Airport was necessary, as both the Irish and American governments thought to use a commercial airport in a neutral country to supply and wage war, or more correctly, genocide, upon the Iraqi people. This was actually happening without informing the public or even asking their permission. By allowing this, the Irish government forfeited its neutrality and made itself complicit in an illegal war against the Iraqi people.

THE CONSTITUTION OF IRELAND, ARTICLE 15, 6, 2:

"No military or armed force, other than a military or armed force raised and maintained by the Oireachtas, shall be raised or maintained for any purpose whatsoever."

At Shannon, the Irish government "maintained", by the act of refuelling US military aircraft and allowing US troops to disembark and shop 'duty free' (even if this was with capitalist intentions), the U.S. military war machine.

ARTICLE 28, 3, 1:

"War shall not be declared and the state shall not participate in any war save with the assent of Dail Eireann."

At the time of our action, the US did not have public or governmental permission to use Shannon Airport in its deployment of troops and munitions to Iraq. What did the Irish government think they were doing at Shannon? Buying souvenirs?

ARTICLE 29, 1:

"Ireland affirms its devotion to the ideal of peace and friendly co-operation amongst nations founded on international justice and morality."

The Irish government was so devoted to the ideal of peace, that it demonstrated this by selling its people, its neutrality, its justice and its morality, to the US dollar. At Shannon, the Irish government not only contravened international law and its own constitution, it lied to its people. Even two previous actions taken by individuals at Shannon failed to stop the Irish government's whorish behaviour!

As a non-violent individual dedicated to a more peaceful existence, I find accusations that our action was violent and anti-American both ignorant and arrogant, to say the least. Whilst in prison, we have been accused of 'destroying the Irish economy' and once again, being 'anti-American'. I find this ludicrous, as one of us is American, and if we could destroy capitalism we would all be delighted and the world would be a better place.

Both the Irish government and the US government put civilians at risk at Shannon. The British government is now doing the same at Prestwick. The first casualty of war is innocence – THEY LIE WE DIE! Which part of the word PEACE don't they understand?

Karen came out of jail only as the first, 'successful' phase of the US/British attack on Iraq was ending in April. It was a difficult moment, politically and personally. She had been in jail on remand for more than two-and-a-half months, and would have stayed longer rather than allow the Irish state to turn her 'loose' for another, cheap form of incarceration – confinement to Irish territory – while she awaited trial for what she regarded as a lawful act. However, she was sick, and not inclined to trust prison doctors. She had been separated from her Catholic Worker comrades for a great deal of her prison time, and had made up her mind that while she wished them well, she was not prepared to start up a community with them. An old friend invited her to come stay in County Sligo, in the northwest of Ireland far from the other four in Dublin. She decided she would do that.

Back in Dublin, Deirdre Clancy was back in her old apartment on the Northside, and Nuin Dunlop was moving around a bit. As Ciaron moved to Kimmage to stay with Damien, he reflected that in one respect, at least, the process had not gone according to his expectations: a Dublin Catholic Worker community had not really evolved, and the women in particular made it clear they were not committed to that particular goal. There remained a lot of affection among the five, but they had given themselves little time for 'community building' before the action. Bonds had built up in prison largely along gender lines, and tensions now emerged along those same lines. No one who heard the sometimes-heated arguments when the group met that spring could have mistaken this for a personality cult around Ciaron O'Reilly. Eventually it became the case that all five of them rarely met, though the tensions mostly settled down.

In June 2003, during a demonstration at Shannon when the Pitstop Ploughshares stayed at the county line, as far as they legally could go, Deirdre met Fintan Lane, a labour historian who was the stalwart of anti-war politics in the southwest city of Cork. Lane too was banned from Clare: had been arrested as part of a trespass at Shannon Airport in

October of 2002, and though he faced only a minor charge he was determined to go to jail, where he would have to serve a 60-day sentence, rather than pay the fine. Lane was an immensely impressive character, with keen intelligence, a gentle manner and matter-of-fact commitment. He saw the same qualities and more in Deirdre, and they soon formed a relationship. He befriended all the group, and was a particularly good confidante for the women. Fintan became a frequent visitor to Dublin, and before long a resident of the capital, a difficult wrench for any Corkman but one he took with typical good grace.

The legal situation for the Pitstop Ploughshares was getting more clear. When they appeared at Ennis District Court in May it emerged that the estimated cost of repairing the plane after their action was an incredible $2.7 million, making rather a mockery of the initial police claim that they had been prevented from doing any serious damage. Mary Kelly's attack on the same plane was now being costed at over $1 million. Even with the ludicrous inflation attached to all costs involving the US military – the bill came on an itemised list from the US Navy that looked very official but lacked any specific costings – it was now clear they had done some serious 'disarmament': the plane itself had not returned to action until May, meaning its services were not used at all in the initial weeks of the attack on Iraq.

This level of damage and the fact that they were pleading not guilty and facing a jury trial at the level of the Circuit Court meant they could face long sentences if convicted. Conceivably, they could go to jail for 10 years. They were scheduled for trial at Ennis Circuit Court in County Clare on June 24th, and Joe Noonan sought more legal aid so he could bring more, and more senior, barristers in to argue the case. (In the Irish system, barristers do the talking in court rather than solicitors once you get beyond the minor courts.)

Noonan also decided it would be unwise to fight the case in County Clare, if it could possibly be avoided. He warned his clients that given the nature of the case and attendant publicity locally, it would be difficult to find dispassionate jury members in the area, bearing in mind the economic dependency of many people, their families and extended families not only on the airport itself but on the multinational businesses that surround it. The presence of these businesses was constantly claimed to be in danger because of anti-war protests at the airport.

It was undoubtedly a strong argument, and when it was presented to Judge Carroll Moran in Ennis Circuit Court, the judge accepted it, announcing on June 17th, with a nod to the attending media, that he did not mean "any slight on the people of Clare." The trial venue would be in Dublin, and with the crush of cases to be heard in the capital's Circuit Criminal Court, and the legal team's intention to seek pre-trial documentation from the state detailing the US military use of Shannon, the prospect of a full trial taking place within 2003 suddenly receded.

Surprisingly, however, Mary Kelly's legal team did not seek a change of venue, and her trial steamed ahead in Ennis in July 2003. It was an extraordinary spectacle: at short notice she and her lawyers had got Ramsey Clark, Scott Ritter and Denis Halliday to come testify on her behalf about the illegality of the war and its consequences. Michael Bermingham, a Dubliner and peace activist who spent most of the first half of 2003 in Baghdad, also testified, over prosecution objections that his evidence was emotive and irrelevant. As the trial's four days went on, however, Judge Moran got tougher on the defence, which is supposed to have wide latitude to present its case. Ritter, for example, was hardly permitted to testify at all.

After legal argument, Judge Moran summed up the case to the jury by, effectively, telling them they had to ignore much of what they had heard. Kelly could not possibly have had a 'lawful excuse' to damage the plane, he said, because the danger it allegedly posed to others was not immediate. The defence under the law could not possibly extend to the circumstances in this case, he said. And faced with the judge's decision on the law, Kelly's barrister, Brendan Nix, had no argument other than an emotional one to put on her behalf. Fortunately, Nix is an extraordinarily evocative speaker, and much to everyone's surprise given the venue and the firm legal ruling, the jury could not reach a verdict, not even by a 10-to-two majority.

Mary Kelly's hung jury was a striking outcome, but some way short of an all-out legal success. Along with some others, Noonan and Giollaiosa Ó Lideadha got down to work, digging into the statute and case law to see if they could secure a better outcome on 'lawful excuse' for the Pitstop Ploughshares, whose case was so similar.

The group was staying visible, largely through the work of Ciaron and Damien, who both proved able PR-generators, despite the media's insistence on keeping the case's profile low. They would hold quite regular anti-war vigils, sometimes daily, in Dublin city centre, often at the Irish Aviation Authority, keeping the focus on Shannon; they met actor Martin Sheen and got a 'presidential pardon' from him; Ciaron's history of Timorese solidarity work meant East Timor's president Xanana Gusmao also met with them supportively; Desmond Tutu did still another meeting. They were putting together an impressive photographic file, though the women were not in all the pictures.

The crucial legal battle began to be fought in the autumn of 2003 before Dublin Circuit Court Judge Joseph Mathews, in what is called the 'discovery' stage of the trial process. The Five's lawyers wanted to get detailed evidence of how the US had been using Shannon Airport, including the periods when it was probably in violation of Irish law in carrying munitions without authorisation, and the use and destinations of troops and equipment going through the airport. They wanted the prosecution to be made to supply that evidence before any trial, rather than the defence having to seek it from Irish and US authorities during that trial, with uncertain results – "pot-luck," one lawyer called it. Most importantly, in securing a ruling that they were entitled to such evidence, they wanted the judge to acknowledge that what the US was up to in Shannon and Iraq was relevant to the case, because 'lawful excuse' could conceivably apply in these circumstances.

At a hearing in December, senior counsel for the defendants Hugh Hartnett set out the argument, backed by copious documentation amassed by Ó Lideatha. The case as Hartnett stated it focused on a few key words in Irish law. The offence with which the five were charged was set down in the Criminal Damage Act of 1991, but the relevant defence to the charge had clearly been amended by another law, somewhat strangely the Non-Fatal Offences Against the Person Act 1997. Part of section 21 of that act was the all-important mouthful:

> If he damaged or threatened to damage the property in question... in order to protect himself or another or property belonging to himself or another, or a right or interest in property which was or which he believed to be vested in himself or another and the act or acts alleged to constitute the offence were reasonable in the circumstances, as he believed them to be.

Intriguingly, the original act had stipulated that the person or property being protected must be "in immediate need of protection," but for whatever reason the amended law had dropped that phrase. If there was really an immediacy requirement here, as Judge Moran had suggested, it was not immediately obvious in the wording of the statutory defence.

And so, Hartnett explained, the facts the defence wanted "are relevant because the jury must assess whether the acts were reasonable in the circumstances, as [the accused] believed them to be, [and so] must take into account whether that person was correct in their assessment of the situation."

Judge Mathews wondered if the jury assessment of whether the person was correct was "objective or subjective".

"It's both, my Lord."

"Both?"

"For the purpose of trial I do not want to seem to be giving too much away, my Lord. What I say is this: it is a subjective test but a jury cannot be deprived of the opportunity of knowing whether the accused person was correct in their assessment. Clearly that must be relevant to whether the accused was being reasonable in their assessment of the situation. Otherwise, my Lord… it would be the stuff of Alice in Wonderland that you could have a debate here as to whether the accused was reasonably correct but that the jury were deprived of the opportunity, and indeed the accused deprived of the opportunity, of knowing whether in fact they were absolutely correct. Or, indeed, absolutely mistaken…

"The matters that we have enquired into involve the status of the plane,… the purpose for which it was there and the intentions held by the owners of the plane for its use."

But, the judge wondered, could they really expect the US government to cough up detailed information about its intentions for the plane's use? Hartnett replied that the question was "another day's work:" all the court could do now, he said, was to address the question of relevance, whatever practical difficulties might follow.

As Hartnett explained, based on clear precedent, the complainant in a criminal trial (that is, the state) is bound to supply any information relevant to the case whether favourable to the prosecution or the accused. If the prosecution cannot obtain evidence, disclosure of which is necessary for the purposes of the defence, the accused may be entitled to have the charges dismissed.

The jury, the defence lawyer insisted, must be in a position when looking at the defendants to assess the objective question: "Were they right?" It could only do that, he said, with hard facts. It would be crazy if the jury got to the deliberation stage and found themselves saying, with an Irish verbal shrug, "sure, maybe this was a chartered flight to Cuba for winter holidays…"

Judge Mathews agreed, and gave an order for disclosure of information about the plane, and about the build-up of US forces through Shannon. The prosecution, while admitting that 'immediate' wasn't in the law any more, insisted there should at least be a clear 'nexus' between the event of damage and the threat that might emanate from the object being damaged. The state's lawyer seemed rather flabbergasted, and stepped a little beyond the usual bounds of propriety that govern how a barrister addresses a judge: "It flies in the face of logic absolutely to propound the notion that because a person has an idea that some thing or some other person may in the future be the cause of injury to other persons or property, that they can act to injure that thing or person for the purposes of preventing something that may happen or may not happen in the future, my Lord. In logic that has no legs and it cannot be dressed up in any way…"

Judge Mathews noticed the strong words, and the lawyer reassured him that he was not accusing him personally of flying in the face of logic. The judge assured him in return that it was open to the state to go to a higher court for 'judicial review' to quash the order. The prosecution seemed to hope the judge could yet be talked out of it: "If I shoot your dog this evening in the belief that he is going to attack my child three days hence…"

Mathews interrupted: "You will say such a judgment would be a licence to commit damage or even a licence to kill at will?"

The prosecutor remembered that it was criminal damage they were discussing: "Well I am not saying kill now, my Lord, but certainly to damage."

Mathews recognised the problem his ruling might pose in principle: could American abortion-clinic bombings be justified under a similar notion? But that was not the issue here: "I am keeping this to the context of which the case is being fought, the statute that the crimes alleged are being based on, and the arguments that are contained in the very clear legal submissions and the legal arguments in open court…. I am afraid," he told the prosecutor, "if my ruling flies in the face of logic, and I know what you mean by what you said, there is another place to go" – i.e. the High Court. "And they will tear me in flames no doubt."

The prosecution made one last effort to change the judge's mind, complaining that the state would be unable to get its hands on the information. Judge Mathews was somewhat incredulous: "So nobody from the state side would know the number of flights which landed at Shannon Airport?"

"No, my Lord."

"Are you serious?"

"Well, no, my Lord..."

"No, seriously, are you serious?" Surely, Judge Mathews suggested, some agency of the state, apart from the office of the Director of Public Prosecutions, could be expected to have or be able to get such data on Shannon. He underlined the importance of some factual basis for the defendants' beliefs under the statutory defence: "Even if the jury accepts the accused believe the acts would help save the lives of innocent people in imminent danger, the jury may be directed to form its own view of whether the acts were reasonable in those perceived circumstances."

The prosecution fought back: "What relevance is it whether one other plane or 5,000 other planes landed at Shannon belonging to the American government?"

Mathews, astonishingly, returned to the abortion-clinic analogy, this time imagining an Irish scenario. "Supposing there was an attack on property and it turned out the property was a room in a clinic where it was alleged unlawful abortions or terminations were being done, could a group of concerned but, maybe, some people would argue, misled citizens damaging that property argue they were trying to stop the destruction of human life yet unborn?" If the accused in such a case sought documents on "what, if any, terminations were carried out, who were the officials who carry out these terminations, what are the stages of pregnancy when it is being carried out, how many people have the clinic helped terminate very late pregnancies," the judge said, "it would hardly be fair for [the prosecution] to argue... 'well, it was only a small waiting room'.... You know, such is a hangar with one aeroplane. There are bigger issues."

It was a comprehensive legal victory for the Pitstop Ploughshares defence team. The prosecution hemmed and hawed for a few weeks, professing to be confused about the precise requirements of the order. When the case returned to his courtroom, Judge Mathews insisted that however wrong he might be, the order was what it was, and he couldn't change it or (he joked in the midst of the British 'dodgy dossier' scandal) "sex it up." The prosecution decided it had no choice but to go to the High Court for 'judicial review' of the judge's decision. At the most optimistic assessment, that could take many months.

The delay was devastating in some ways for the defendants, especially Karen and Nuin, who had hopes of being able to get free of a criminal process so far from their homes. However, it did have the consequence of leading Judge Mathews to grant some relaxation in bail conditions, with the possibility of brief foreign travel as long as there was plenty of advanced warning to the police and various check-ups adhered to while abroad. The County Clare ban was shrunk to a much closer radius around the airport.

Ciaron O'Reilly made the most of that change in June 2004, when George Bush came to Ireland (then holding the rotating presidency of the European Union) for a quick summit with EU leaders. The Bush visit offered the best opportunity in well over a year for high-visibility, well-attended protest – and, unfortunately, for further displays of the divisions in the ranks of the broad anti-war community in Ireland, as separate groups organized demonstrations in Shannon where Bush was landing and near where he was staying, as well as in Dublin and elsewhere.

Ciaron decided that Bush's presence in the luxury hotel at the medieval-looking Dromoland Castle offered a perfect opportunity for creative protest. He conceived 'MacBush', in which a procession of protesters would carry cardboard-cutout trees, bearing names of Iraqi dead (mostly children, with a note of their ages and cause of death) as far as they could go towards the castle – like Birnam Wood come to Dunsinane in the final act of *Macbeth*. Caoimhe Butterly, a late addition to the cast when the first actress was arrested flying into Shannon, would do a Lady

Macbeth soliloquy, and O'Reilly himself donned a US Army uniform, whiteface make-up and some gore for his locks to become Banquo's ghost, ready to haunt MacBush for his many murders. Another friend put on a witch costume, ready to cast Bush out of Ireland.

Security for the visit bordered on the insane, with locals for miles around being issued special passes and most of the Irish Army's equipment, including small tanks, drafted into the area. A special pre-fab detention centre, quickly dubbed 'Shantanamo' by activist wits, was erected for the occasion.

O'Reilly and a couple of dozen friends gathered in a nearby village, ready to walk out the narrow country road toward the castle. On the same day the Irish Anti-War Movement had secured police permission to approach the castle, though still stopping about a mile away. Ciaron was sure the 'MacBush' procession – joined by some would-be IAWM demonstrators who were tired of waiting for the buses to arrive from Dublin – would not get even that far, as the police would distinguish it from the 'official' IAWM march, which was being bussed to a cordoned-off position before walking a short way down the empty road.

Amazingly, however, the security largely evaporated. 'MacBush' passed unharassed through miles of rolling Irish countryside. The IAWM buses, with a few hundred protesters, passed it by. As 'MacBush' walked on for miles, it became clear that it would reach the same police lines that the IAWM had so carefully negotiated: the police hadn't distinguished at all among the various and not necessarily mutually friendly emanations of the anti-war movement. What was worse, once the buses reached their destination and unloaded, the 'MacBush' procession and the IAWM were converging from two different points on to the same final, narrow stretch of road, absolutely simultaneously. The IAWM march leaders stretched their lead banner across the road just in time to split 'MacBush' in two, seeming to absorb at least half the 'trees' into the larger march, with a few more out in front. The rapidity of the move and the sudden noise of the IAWM march seemed like a deliberate effort to disrupt 'MacBush' or at least prevent it from leading the whole crowd down the road before the assembled media cameras.

Ciaron was furious, and tried to get the trees through, but his megaphone was no match for those of the IAWM and its assembled ranks. In annoyance he threw a stealthy forearm into the back of a Socialist Workers Party stalwart who was leading the megaphone chants: it wasn't a punch, not even really an elbow, more a jostle for attention; but even in rather fraught circumstances it was an act of physical aggression from a professed pacifist. Ciaron, even as he was displaying the wit and creativity that made him such a potentially attractive figure in the movement, couldn't stop himself from displaying the anger that helped make him such a divisive one. Perhaps, in his military uniform, it was an excess of method acting.

Ciaron argued with IAWM chairman Richard Boyd-Barrett, calling him a "fuckin' moderate." Boyd-Barrett called O'Reilly a "God-ist".

Ultimately, the IAWM, largely through the accident of setting up their stage 100 feet from the police line, allowed time and space to 'MacBush' in the face of the cops, and the spectacle of costumed protesters gathered in front of ranks of police hogged much of the media coverage of Bush's visit, in Ireland and abroad. However, the other kind of spectacle O'Reilly made of himself left a further legacy of bitterness in the diminishing ranks of the anti-war movement.

Meanwhile, the lawyers for the state and the defence were in negotiation to see if they could resolve the 'discovery' question short of the long and costly 'judicial review' process. Happily, they could do so, with the state getting out of seeking the information that only the US government could provide, but agreeing to get and share information on the number of troops and flights that had gone though Shannon, and flown over Ireland, in a set period, three months prior to the event (shorter than the period specified in the original order) and to answer questions about how and when the state inspected and/or authorised such flights. Such information, much of it publicly available anyway, could prove useful, but it was less important than the fact that they had successfully argued that the 'lawful excuse' defence was 'statable' under the circumstances of this case.

That was just as well, because Mary Kelly's long-delayed second trial in the Ennis Circuit Court, in October 2004, ended in failure. Kelly bravely represented herself after falling out with her lawyers, and with the help of dedicated lay friends and advisers she put the argument for 'lawful excuse' as powerfully, learnedly and coherently as she could. This time around, Judge Carroll Moran was much more aggressive in rejecting witnesses who would talk about the war – this time Daniel Ellsberg had joined Denis Halliday and others, but none got a chance to speak. And when Judge Moran got around to charging the jury he shot Kelly down in no uncertain terms:

> The law is that lawful excuse must be in defence of a person or of property and that the threat must be immediate, while the self-defence must also be immediate… The threat has to be immediate to the person and in this case, therefore, anything to do with the war in Iraq or the US military use of Shannon Airport is not relevant to the charge and there is no basis on those issues for the lawful excuse to the charge of criminal damage.

Kelly was convicted, despite two jurors holding out for acquittal, and ended up with a suspended sentence. The Pitstop Ploughshares, now set for trial in March 2005, two years and a month after their action, were hoping for better.

Chapter 7

The Trials Begin

JOE NOONAN HAD WARNED THE FIVE ABOUT PRE-TRIAL MEDIA attention. The women were largely inclined to err on the side of caution. Damien Moran and Ciaron O'Reilly, however, pressed ahead with low-key but persistent efforts to generate support in the lead-up to their case at last being fully heard in court. The Pitstop Ploughshares website got a snappy but legally provocative name, waron-trial.com; a programme of events for the period of the court-case was planned under the 'War on Trial' title, with American speaking guests including Kathy Kelly, Thomas Gumbleton, auxiliary bishop of Detroit, and Kelly Dougherty, a young woman who was active in Iraq Veterans Against the War.

Furthermore, in late February 2005 Damien and Ciaron launched an initiative that combined moral principles with an attempt to gain public-ity outside the confines of the criminal case, while keeping the focus on Shannon.

The US military's reliance on the airport had not lessened in the two years since the action. On the contrary, in 2004, 158,549 US troops passed through the airport on 1,502 flights – more than four a day, mainly civil-ian charter aircraft. Those troop numbers were 26 per cent higher than in 2003. In addition, Irish officials granted permission for 753 military aircraft to land, and 816 aircraft carrying munitions.

Something needed to be done to weaken this link in the chain of murder and corruption connecting Washington and Iraq. Damien had the idea that Shannon should be publicised as a place where US soldiers with doubts about the war should seek asylum while their planes refuel, rather than simply wandering through the duty-free.

Ciaron and Damien were joined by Deirdre for a press conference on the subject. A couple of Irish parliamentarians and the remarkable anti-war activist, former Irish Army Commandant Ed Horgan – acknowledging that as a soldier he found it hard to advise other soldiers effectively to desert – added their voices to the call. It failed to generate much interest in the mainstream media, but internet publicity for it produced a trickle of interest from American soldiers considering their options.

There were bits and pieces of other Pitstop Ploughshares publicity. A new left-leaning magazine, *Village*, was edited by Vincent Browne, a veteran investigative reporter and editor, as well as a qualified barrister, who had long believed that the media took 'sub judice' restrictions much further than the law or the courts would actually demand. Moreover, the facts of the Pitstop Ploughshares case were not in dispute. Shortly before the trial, *Village* published a substantial interview by journalist John Byrne with Ciaron O'Reilly, in which Ciaron went into some detail about the action and its justifications.

Outside the internet, where Indymedia continued to be a rich source of supportive material on the case, this was a rare intervention. Only a short solidarity 'occupation' of the Irish embassy in London a few days before the trial gained much attention. The wait now in the media and elsewhere was for the trial to begin in the Dublin Circuit Criminal Court. Judge Mathews would not be presiding, and his ruling 15 months earlier on 'discovery', while helpful and encouraging, would not be binding on whoever took charge of the trial. The defence team's strategy would be not to argue the 'lawful excuse' question straight away, but to keep their legal arguments in reserve and the question at least open, so that the defendants would get the best possible chance to offer wide-ranging testimony about their backgrounds, actions and motivations. On the face of it, a jury of 12 ordinary people, after all, would be making a bit of a leap to find themselves siding with the likes of Ciaron O'Reilly. They would have to be introduced to these five good people as well as being introduced to the arguments, so that by the end of the trial, they could say, yes, there is reasonable cause to think that these defendants honestly believed they damaged this property to save lives in Iraq, and that belief was reasonable in the circumstances as they perceived them to be. But of course, in order for them to be able to come to that conclusion, it was likely that the judge – unlike Judge Moran in Ennis –would ultimately have to instruct them that such a conclusion was at least possible to draw from the application of the law to this case.

The defendants had agreed that on each day of the trial, a procession would move off from O'Connell Street 60 to 90 minutes in advance, for the 20-minute walk down to the 'Four Courts' complex where the proceedings would take place. A couple of years previously, an enormous, 300-meter-tall metal spire had been erected in the pedestrian island in the middle of the capital's main street, near to the General Post Office that had acted as a headquarters for the main rebel group in the 1916 Rising. The Spire's merits as a piece of public art were much debated, but its power as a civic focus was indisputable.

On Monday, March 7th, 2005, Ciaron O'Reilly's 45th birthday, about 120 people gathered at the Spire shortly after 9am, and set off to wind their way westward through the city. Carmen Trotta was over from the New York Catholic Worker to coordinate much of the support activity, and he tried to keep the procession single file, silent and commemorative of the war's victims. Irish sociability has a way of taking over, however, especially in such exciting circumstances, and soon people were drifting into pairs to talk. Once at the courthouse it turned into a real talkative session. As it happened, one learned as one talked and listened to people that there was a substantial minority of non-Irish people in this crowd, over from America mainly – like the extended family of Gradys from upstate New York, Catholic Worker activists already planning their afternoon tourist itinerary. Bishop Gumbleton had missed the procession because his flight from the US was delayed, but Joe Murray, executive director of AfrI, drove the vigorous 75-year-old straight to the courts. There were friends from Britain too, most visibly two old friends of Karen and Ciaron, Japanese nuns from the Nipponzan Myōhōji Buddhist Temple in Milton Keynes, England, leading out the crowd with their drums, then taking up positions at the corner of the courthouse to keep up the rhythm of prayer.

It was hard to hear the speeches against the morning traffic, but the silent hand-holding circle of five defendants said all that needed to be said. Suddenly someone gave them a message that their lawyers wanted them inside, and they literally ran off into the complex.

No matter how long and hard you anticipate an event like this, there are often elements that still manage to confuse you. Outside the courthouse it was hard to find anyone, for example, who seemed confident about what precisely was going to happen today, and where. Deirdre's partner Fintan Lane and a sympathetic journalist, neither of them frequenters of the court system, decided to go ask at the information desk just off the main rotunda about what was happening to the five. The distracted clerk said they would be in Court 2, not before 11am. This seemed a bit odd, since Court 2 is a huge fancy one near that grand domed space, where you wouldn't expect to find a mere Circuit Court sitting. As 11am approached, they found out from a friendly photographer that the Court 2 case involved a group of five guys who had let out a whoop of approval after an acquittal last week, and were now being dragged in to purge their contempt before the not-amused judge. It was a timely reminder to mind your manners in court. But what about the Pitstop Ploughshares? Ah, the *Shannon* Five – the name that the legal system had adopted for them. They were outside and around the corner in Court 24.

The word was spread and supporters poured, then squeezed, into a small courtroom. There they found the defendants perched on a bench and Judge Michael White warning a roomful of potential jurors, by a remote audio link, that the alleged crime in this case related to the Iraq war, and therefore if they had strong feelings about that war, they should disqualify themselves. For whatever reason, as they filed one by one into the courtroom, two potential jurors did approach the judge and disqualify themselves before they could be sworn in. Another two got into the box, but before they could swear the oath, the prosecution objected to them, on the standard though unstated grounds that they looked like working-class young men, and therefore apparently predisposed to acquit.

The magic number of 12 was quickly reached, nine women and three men, as ordinary and decent looking as you could hope for. Then the judge told the jury and defendants that the trial would start tomorrow, in he-didn't-know-what-court, and before he-didn't-know-what-judge – either himself, Judge Frank O'Donnell or Judge Donagh McDonagh. And then, before it had barely begun, Day One was done, until 10.30am Tuesday.

Some members of the legal profession and judiciary do get to be public figures in Ireland, but Circuit Court judges are rarely among them, apart from occasional flare-ups of publicity when they make a particularly dramatic sentencing statement or find some reason to criticise the government from the bench. So the five and their friends didn't have much luck digging up information about the prospective judges: such reputations that the judges had focussed on the lengths of their sentences, not their legal philosophies or political connections. Ciaron's birthday celebrations had to proceed amid a welter of ignorant speculation about what might be expected of Judge Whoever in the coming days.

On Tuesday morning they discovered that the judge in question would be Frank O'Donnell, a round-faced rather ruddy oldish man perched under a not-particularly well kept curly white wig. His manner was easy-going: O'Donnell's courtroom, it was quickly clear, would not be especially formal, despite the barristers in their black gowns and, mostly, wigs. (The senior counsel for the prosecution, Conor Devally, was inclined to leave his wig off, seeing it as a colonial holdover.) The array of lawyers was unusual for this level of court. Devally was assisted by two junior counsel, but it was on the defence side that the double row of gowned lawyers got particularly crowded. Joe Noonan, sitting quietly in an ordinary suit just under the judge's bench, had secured the services of three top senior counsel (two fewer than five defendants could have claimed under the state's free legal aid scheme): the tall, stout Hugh Hartnett was representing Damien Moran and Ciaron O'Reilly; the smooth Michael O'Higgins was looking after Nuin Dunlop and Deirdre Clancy; and Brendan Nix, moustachioed like Rumpole of the Bailey, whose oratorical skills had helped save Mary Kelly from conviction first time around, was Karen Fallon's senior. Giollaiosa Ó Lideadha, the junior counsel who had worked so long on this case, sat behind Hartnett, with two other juniors beside him. Barristers in Ireland never move from their positions – they simply stand in place when they're talking – and they communicate to the witnesses, judge and the jury, all arrayed around them on heightened platforms, everything from pleasure to pressure with voice, gesture or posture.

The prosecution's case was, on the face of it, simple. It had to prove that the damage took place and was done by these people, then it had to fend off attempts to defend that damage in law, keeping the war out of the discussion as much as possible. (To this purpose the prosecution consistently referred to the plane as a Boeing 737, which indeed it was, but modified for the military's purposes.) The prosecution program was a simple matter of coordinating a procession through the witness stand of airport managers, policemen and a US Navy officer who was in charge of the plane while it was being repaired and could testify that it was not, in fact, the property of Deirdre Clancy, Nuin Dunlop, Karen Fallon, Damien Moran and Ciaron O'Reilly to do with as they pleased. The defence team, while cross-examining those witnesses, had to make sure all of them were pressed on the US military presence at the airport and the failure of the Irish authorities to investigate its nature. And if they got a chance they'd mention the war and George W. Bush. Brendan

Nix seemed to take particular pleasure in enunciating the five syllables of that hated name, a grand flourish of a disapproving finger ending with a poke in the "Bush."

The team had to be careful with Sergeant Michael O'Connell, the policeman who had been in the hangar when the five entered. He looked grey and nervous in the witness box, and could elicit sympathy from the jury if he was put under too much pressure. His account, especially of how the defendants had shouted and run past him, and of his efforts to disarm them, did not tally with their own recollections. But the discrepancies were probably not of great significance. It was important to get him to acknowledge that he was comforted by Ciaron, and he did that – establishing a tone for the action that was more in keeping with their version of events, and one that they could build upon when it was the defendants' own turn to take the stand. Moreover, the testimony of the other gardaí was full of mentions of O'Connell's distressed state in the hangar, which must surely plant questions in jurors' minds about the total reliability of his memory of the night, however honest it undoubtedly was.

By Wednesday, March 9th, things were starting to get interesting. The defence pointed out a discrepancy between Detective Sergeant Michael Houlihan's notes of his interview with Ciaron O'Reilly and the transcript of the taped interview. The notes quoted Ciaron as saying that the Statement of Faith "justified" the action; in reality, as the tape showed, Ciaron said the statement "explained" the action. The significance of this correction would not become clear until the time was ripe for the defence barristers to outline to judge and, hopefully, jury that this action was not "justified" by religious and political conviction, as powerful as they were, but by law.

The defence made its first significant move in that direction when, just before noon on that Wednesday Hugh Harnett questioned Garda Denis Swift, who had discovered, and dismantled, the shrine outside the hangar. Hartnett asked Swift to pull items from the shrine from the evidence bag: the two videos and the photographs given to the defendants by Kathy Kelly. Hartnett wanted these items given to the jury as exhibits. The prosecution said they were irrelevant. The judge wondered if there was evidence about their provenance. It was time for a legal argument between barristers about the admissibility of this material – the sort of argument that juries aren't allowed to witness. The jurors were sent from the courtroom and the debate began.

Hartnett stated frankly that not only did he believe this material should be available to the jury, but that he might well ask the jury to view the videotapes, which went to the question of the defendants' state of mind. He began to "open the law" on the defence argument, replaying a part of the submission the defence had made in the pre-trial hearing to Judge Mathews. He explained that Section 6 of the Criminal Damage Act 1991, as amended by Section 21 of the Non-Fatal Offences against the Person Act 1997, set a subjective test, in which an accused's honest belief that he was acting to protect the life or property of himself or another was the key. "It is immaterial if a belief is justified or not if it is honestly held" was the wording in the original statute. Thus, he said, material was relevant if it had led a defendant to form a certain view. In this light, even the actual provenance of the photos was irrelevant if the accused believed them to be of Iraqi children, Hartnett said.

The next defence barrister, Michael O'Higgins, chimed in, saying material from the 'shrine' had a "physical and temporal connection to the very core of the case." He said the defendants were motivated by the "appalling and horrific injuries visited on non-combatants" and by what was likely again to happen to non-combatants. He said the jury was entitled to see this evidence, though the jury was of course not bound to conclude that the defendants held such an honest belief.

Brendan Nix joined the chorus, saying that if, for example, in relation to a firearms charge, a video had been found offering training in illegal use of firearms, it would have been displayed by the State "in glorious color." He went on to observe that the prosecution had introduced into evidence photographs of the graffiti outside the hangar, and the inscriptions on the tools used in the action. So why not the contents of the shrine and of the video?

Prosecuting lawyer Conor Devally needed to draw a line, one that would ensure that the considerable journalistic and argumentative skills of John Pilger weren't going to be added to the defence case. He defended the state's failure to include the 'shrine' material as exhibits in the case. He said if the videos had shown, for example, the planning of this act or prior acts by the defendants either consistent or inconsistent with this act he would have provided them. He added if the jurors were to be asked to view the videos, they should also have to read the Bible and the Koran, and perhaps all the other material the defendants read over a period of years that led them to form their views. The question, he said, is not whether they influenced the accused – because that could lead to an unlimited body of evidence – the question was relevance.

Devally went on to what everyone was starting to call "the larger question," saying that apart from the "subjective test," there were objective standards in the statute, "in order to defend another." He said this was not a case where someone was leaping to the defence of someone immediately under threat. Devally warned that by the defence's interpretation, you could extrapolate the section of the act to a "limitless political degree." It would allow, for instance, the burning of a drug dealer's home in order to prevent future harm to children. It involved predicting the future, taking matters into one's own hands, and was illogical and untenable. He said the state did not deny the five's "honest belief." He said "nobody is putting their consciences on trial," and the trial could not explore "a bottomless well of influences."

"This court cannot go that route," Devally said. Then he cleverly and subtly introduced the question of the defendants' agenda, as seen outside the court: "we cannot put the war on trial here."

Hartnett said that while Mr Devally had cited "immediacy," the statute had actually removed that word in its 1997 amendment. Judge

O'Donnell, however, said he could scarcely believe the subjective test could have such power. "With all due respect to village idiots wherever they may be," the judge said, "you couldn't give them the right to burn their rich neighbour's car because they honestly believed him to be stealing from them."

The argument was interrupted by lunch, but then, still leaving the jury outside, it dragged well into the afternoon, with Devally – presumably sensing from the 'village idiot' line that Judge O'Donnell was going to shoot down the defence – saying that the argument had widened and should be pursued further. The defence, however, could sense the same thing, and insisted that only the shrine material was now at issue and, in Hartnett's words, "we should not jump hurdles before we reach them." The right time for the court to decide the broader issue of the legitimacy of the defence under the statute in this case, O'Higgins declared hopefully, was when it had heard all the evidence. Running further ahead than the defence had perhaps hoped to go at this stage, he tried to reassure O'Donnell that 'honest belief' was a necessary but not sufficient defence under the statute, and under case law that showed juries were entitled to use their common sense as to whether an action was proportionate or reasonable. As for 'immediacy,' it was simply not in the law any more. If there was a defence in law that perhaps unwittingly offered too much scope for accused people, then it was up to the legislature to correct its mistake, not up to the courts to avoid its implications.

Devally said he was not deferring the greater argument. This defence, he said, was simply not available. The question of the defendants' honest belief might arise in sentencing, but not in assessing their guilt or innocence: the 1997 amendment, he said, was a technical adjustment that couldn't go as far as the defence was suggesting. Any wider interpretation, he said, would make these not just defences but charters. As far as the prosecution was concerned, he said, the state conceded the defendants' honest belief – there would be no claim that they were just pretending!

At last, Judge O'Donnell said the amendment of the act was clear, but that he was going to rule simply on the shrine contents: "I don't know the parentage" of the items, he said. "The mere fact that they were proximate, brought there, doesn't confer any authenticity on them…. I'm not going to admit evidence simply because I was asked, and simply because it was there." The shrine items were not going to go to the jury as exhibits.

The bigger issue, he said significantly, was: "where do we go from here?"

And that portentous question more or less brought Wednesday's proceedings to an end, without the jury having heard any more evidence. The arguments, while technical, had kept the crowded courtroom (crowded, that is, apart from the empty jury box) riveted for most of the day. When it finished there was an outbreak of amateur expertise that carried over to that night's busy public meeting in town. The undoubtedly biased 'expert' consensus was that the defence had made a great series of points, with O'Higgins a particularly cool and admirable advocate – but that the judge's comments so far were a worry.

Judge O'Donnell began Thursday morning in a hurry. This trial that everyone had agreed should last little more than a week had already turned, by its fourth day, into one of those series of interminable arguments that particularly annoy jurors because they can't hear them. He wanted the jury's ordeal in their back room to be ended as soon as possible, and to that end he wanted to hear the legal submissions on the 'lawful excuse' defence so he could make a ruling.

The defence didn't want to do that, and they seemed prepared to stand firm on the subject – three senior counsel being more top-price wigs than a Circuit Court judge is used to confronting. Hartnett insisted, again, that the time to debate the law was before final arguments and the judge's charge to the jury. The judge frankly worried aloud that in those circumstances the defendants would get on the stand and start sharing their 'honest belief' about Iraq. He seemed to suggest he would resist such evidence. "Let's get pushing along now," the judge said.

Hartnett said there would be other witnesses too, including a logistics expert, and that the witnesses' relevance would be considered one by one as they appeared. O'Donnell again was quite open about not liking the sound of that. He didn't want this to turn, he said, "into a political trial." Who would these other witnesses be?

Before Hartnett could answer, O'Higgins jumped in to express another concern. What if the first defendant due in the stand, Ciaron O'Reilly, were to give a line of testimony that was then closed down by the judge, ruling against the relevance of 'honest belief'? That would mean that other defendants, including his own clients Deirdre Clancy and Nuin Dunlop, would be very much pre-restricted in terms of their own testimony. Wouldn't it better to, say, call all the evidence in the jury's absence, then get a ruling on its relevance? (Eyes rolled at the idea of the delay this would cause, just as O'Higgins presumably meant them to roll.) Or better yet, couldn't they just run all the evidence before the jury, and then the judge could rule if the defence applied or not? Yes, indeed, that latter one would be his own preferred scenario, O'Higgins said, with no apparent understatement.

He hadn't a hope. Devally said such a scenario would contaminate the trial with evidence that, in the end, would prove to be inadmissible. The judge agreed, saying it would be a "total waste of time" as well as contaminating the jury. Judge O'Donnell clearly wanted to take the bull by the horns – any defence witnesses that were proposed other than the defendants, he said, would have their potential evidence scrutinised and relevance debated before they spoke before the jury.

The arguments were still hopping around, unresolved, when the judge decided to bring the jury back in and allow the defence to call Ciaron O'Reilly. Ciaron, in his usual loose, dark, casual clothes, his dreadlocks tied back, stepped up into the box and affirmed, rather than swore, than his evidence would be true. With his own barrister, Hugh Hartnett, throwing the questions, Ciaron described his history and that of the Catholic Worker movement, founded in the 1930s by Dorothy Day, with three main elements: to be a faith-based community of prayer and work; to do works such as sheltering the homeless, feeding the hungry, visiting prisoners; and to bear public witness against war and preparations for war.

He came to Ireland in April 2002, working first with young heroin addicts at Clancy barracks and then in the city centre, then for the last two years working at a wet-shelter for homeless people. As for his beliefs about the Iraq war, he explained that in 1990, during the preparation for the previous attack on Iraq, he was working "at a soup kitchen and shelter in Washington DC, for women and children, many of whom were – "

Judge O'Donnell's discomfort finally got the better of him, and he interrupted Ciaron: "I'm not going to allow him to go into his whole political agenda."

Ciaron smiled and said, "I've no agenda."

Defendants usually have fairly broad licence to talk about their backgrounds, and after some discussion, the judge allowed Ciaron to return to his time in DC, during the build-up to the first Iraq war. The US government, he recalled, was going to create a lot more homelessness and death through its action. Then came the aftermath, he said: "The war did not end with the end of the 'first Gulf war', but continued with sanctions to strangle the people of Iraq."

As a Christian, he said, he saw that the requirement to feed the poor etc was being blocked by sanctions. And US and UK air forces were still bombing Iraq. He met in the 1990s with people like Kathy Kelly and Ramsey Clark who told him about these things. The sanctions, he said, had "unleashed plagues of gastroenteritis, cholera and typhoid."

Judge O'Donnell interrupted, again asking, "What belief is it we're talking about?"

O'Reilly said the people of Iraq were unnecessarily suffering and dying, especially the children, because of sanctions enforced by the US Navy. He cited Denis Halliday's description of the sanctions as genocidal.

Later, in Ireland, he said, he met Michael Bermingham and Caoimhe Butterly, who had been in Iraq and told him that Saddam Hussein and Iraq's government were doing quite well. Who was dying were the very old, the very young and the very poor. And people in Iraq were now in total fear about what was coming next.

Judge O'Donnell interrupted again.

Hartnett said the law and justice demanded that his client "be permitted some time to explain his – "

Judge O'Donnell interrupted Hartnett: "I'm not going to have him promoting an agenda."

Resuming after a bit more argument, O'Reilly said he believed a lot more killings were to come. "I felt an obligation as a Christian to act." He met Kathy Kelly at a festival for St Brigid in Kildare. "She was on her way to Baghdad to put her body between the bombs – "

Judge O'Donnell interrupted again, and sent the jury away.

Judge O'Donnell said "this man" could not indulge in a wide-ranging anti-war programme that had nothing to do with the charges. "He's conducting a propaganda campaign" in relation to the war, the judge said.

Hartnett chose this moment to press again for the submission of the shrine videotapes, in particular, as evidence in the defence case.

Judge O'Donnell said he would rule on that now.

Giollaiosa Ó Lideadha stood up to explain the content of the John Pilger documentary, including its explanation of the role played by the US Navy, whose plane the defendants had damaged.

Hartnett threw in a cheeky reminder to the judge: the prosecution was here to conduct the case for the state, he said, while "Your Lordship is here as an impartial observer."

"I am not going to allow this court to be turned into a political platform," O'Donnell replied. He said he believed the tapes were designed to turn people against war in Iraq. That was a legitimate function outside the court, he said, but not inside.

Devally, the prosecutor, stood up for the first time since Ciaron had taken the stand, and asked if he might contribute.

"Of course, I'm waiting for you!" Judge O'Donnell said. There was an audible intake of breath around the courtroom. Had the judge really just told the prosecutor that he had been waiting for him to make an objection?

Nix rose to his feet with all the indignation he could muster, and that was plenty. "That was a most unfortunate comment," he said, since it indicated that the judge believed he had to conduct the state's case for it. There was a heated exchange in which the judge said to Nix, "Control yourself."

Nix found new heights of indignation and demanded the withdrawal of the comment and the implication that he was out of control.

Judge O'Donnell said, "I apologise, most profusely. Are you comfortable now?"

Among the spectators there was confusion and disbelief – at the tetchy and personal nature of these exchanges, and at the judge's open hostility to the basis of the defence case. Devally pressed on, asking the judge to rule now on whether the defence had any basis in law, "if it's in the case or not – otherwise we're putting the cart before the horse." O'Higgins predictably differed, saying that defendants didn't need the judge's permission at this point to run a certain defence. It was a "fundamental misconception," he said, to view any expression of political opinions as turning the trial into a political event. The central issue was the "circumstances as the accused believed them to be," and these circumstances were the imminent destruction and loss of life in Iraq. And in looking at that the five were of course informed by what went on before.

Judge O'Donnell said the issue in this case wasn't about O'Reilly's honestly held beliefs. The issue, he said, would boil down to the statutory defence, "in order to protect life or property," and to "what they were about down there" in the Shannon hangar. He ruled that the tapes and photos would not be shown, but that "you can refer to them." He called the jury back in and Ciaron was on show again.

Ciaron testified about the quick formation of the group and the build-up to their action, including his part in previous protests at Shannon, the evident inactivity of the Irish authorities about possible contraventions of Irish law, and the Kildare festival.

They went into the airfield and toward the hangar, he said, looking for an opportunity to "enflesh the prophesy" of swords into ploughshares. He said they were carrying gardening implements and simple household hammers, and intended to disable the airplane, in order to preserve life in Iraq, and property, hospitals, water-treatment works, what sustains life.

Ciaron's barrister, Hartnett, posed one question that provided an opportunity for Ciaron to explicitly challenge Sergeant O'Connell's testimony. Had they had entered the hangar noisily or surreptitiously?

O'Reilly said: "We were going into an area where we thought people would be armed – cautiously, silently, in a very considered fashion." He said they hoped to disable the plane so it would play no further role in the killing of people. He said the act was also "invitational… We hoped other people would join us – the guards would have been good."

Now it was Devally's turn to cross-examine O'Reilly. He had been involved since college in Christian activities, consistently since that time, hadn't he?

"I guess I would consider myself as having a vocation rather than a career," Ciaron replied, adding that "the pacifist ethic" was central to his Christianity.

Devally said it had "brought you into conflict with authorities."

"No more than Jesus I guess."

Devally began to follow this up when Hartnett interrupted, objecting to this questioning and the jury was sent out. Clearly annoyed, Hartnett said that Devally knew well that there was a bar on reference to past offences, including by implication or innuendo, which was worse. The judge told Devally he wasn't allowed to do that.

With the jury back, Devally moved on to painting O'Reilly as a publicity seeker, mentioning the *Would You Believe* TV show.

"Am I shy? No, I'm not shy," O'Reilly said. He said he believed in free speech, and reluctantly cooperated with the mainstream media. He said he was trained as a teacher, to educate, to stimulate, and to learn things himself. He tried to make a joke about Shannon, saying it was the first time in his life he had broken a window, "which was remarkable given how much cricket and football I played on the street."

As for generating a public reaction: "If that resonated with other people, that would be great. If it resonated with many people we could stop this war." They hoped to disable the plane, and to initiate an unpredictable chain of events, but also to answer the question: "How can I be human in this situation if I don't act?"

Devally got the mattock taken out of the bag and handed to O'Reilly – ostensibly to ID it as his tool; but it meant Ciaron, this large and rather scary-looking man, held this large and rather scary-looking object on his lap through a long stretch of testimony. You could see jurors' eyes constantly wander to it as Devally continued his questioning.

"Was it your purpose to make a point?"

"My purpose was to disable the US Navy warplane."

"Were you thinking of making a point? Did you think your action was likely to become known, to be a nuisance?"

"I was hoping it would be an inspiration."

"Did you think it would be a nuisance to those it did not inspire?"

O'Reilly said it made overt what had been covert, the militarization of a civilian airport.

After a break for lunch, Devally again worked hard to paint O'Reilly as a publicity seeker and his action as essentially symbolic, aimed at delivering a message rather than protecting life. O'Reilly said the shrine was set up quite quickly, and the graffiti on the hangar was to name the building for what it was, a pitstop of death, and to make a statement that the war stops here, "our complicity with it." That meant his own personal complicity, that of the people actively involved in its prosecution, and "our silence in letting that happen." To name the hangar, "to reveal its true nature," might be helpful to others.

Devally said they had employed symbols. "We're Catholic, we deal in symbols," O'Reilly said. This prompted the judge to intervene: "Sounds like Lourdes" – referring to the French pilgrimage site where sick and lame Catholics hope for miracle cures.

"No one has walked," Hartnett quipped. "Yet."

Devally continued, asking O'Reilly about their expectation of arrest. O'Reilly cited the precedent of the Berlin Wall, when guards and soldiers joined in the wall's demolition. Devally asked if he was surprised to be arrested. "Disappointed," O'Reilly said.

It took a long round of questioning before it was entirely clear what Devally was getting at: not only the action, but the arrest and the criminal proceedings that were bound to follow were all an effort to generate anti-war publicity. After some argument in the absence of the jury, Devally was allowed to read from an interview that Ciaron had done with Amy Goodman, in which he said the group was planning "to put the war on trial" – a phrase guaranteed to irritate Judge O'Donnell.

O'Reilly said the phrase did not refer to these proceedings but to activities outside the trial. Devally said O'Reilly had done the action in order to publicize his views and to maximize opposition to the war, and it was calculated to bring about his trial.

"It was a matter of politics, and this was an expression of your politics."

"It was an expression of my faith as a Christian."

By the time Ciaron was finished, the trial had been delayed considerably and the defence was in a hurry to present a key expert witness who was planning to fly back to England: Geoffrey Oxlee, a military-logistics expert. In the absence of the jury, Giollaiosa Ó Lideadha briefly explained the rationale: Oxlee could give evidence as to whether damaging a plane in this case could properly be viewed as protecting lives and property. He said if there was any doubt the evidence could be heard first in the absence of the jury.

Devally said he didn't know the witness's provenance, or how anyone could have expertise on this matter.

Judge O'Donnell was back in the mood to be annoyed at the defence. "At some stage or another this issue was going to have to be faced," he said. He said the testimony was not relevant. He said the lives and property had to be something that the action was capable of protecting, and capable of protecting in a concrete manner. This witness's evidence would be nebulous. He said neither the amendment, nor the act as amended, was designed to hand over to individuals the bailiwick of the Irish government in terms of its attitudes to other people's wars.

This sounded almost like a lament about what he was being subjected to, rather than an actual ruling – but if it were the latter, it seemed not only to rule out testimony before he had heard much about it, but also to decree, before hearing full legal argument, that the statutory defence couldn't possibly apply in this case, and that this had something to do with government policy. The junior barristers on the defence side were scribbling furiously. Hartnett stood up to complain that Judge O'Donnell had ruled on the interpretation of the statute before receiving submissions – i.e. arguments from the lawyers. O'Higgins joined in to ask if the judge was now ruling out the defence of lawful excuse. Judge O'Donnell said he wasn't, but it was hard to square that with what he had just said. Nix rose to say that when in doubt the statute was to be construed in favour of the accused person. Both Nix and O'Higgins made applications for the discharge of the jury – i.e. for a mistrial on the basis of the way the judge had handled this few minutes of argument.

Judge O'Donnell said: "I feel the undertones of an agenda, and from the outline of what I've got I felt this was a big brick in the agenda, that had nothing to do with the defence…" He appeared to be referring to the Oxlee testimony, but again his statement was so broad it sent shock-waves through the courtroom. He adjourned the court for the day on that Thursday afternoon, sending the jury home for the weekend in anticipation of a day's legal argument on Friday, and the buzz of excitement again lasted all evening.

The problem with seeking a mistrial in these circumstances is that you've got to convince a judge to rule against himself. What's more, in this case it was clearly imperative to convince O'Donnell that his own comments and behavior couldn't stand up to scrutiny – because if he continued in the same vein the defence would be crippled. The pain of having to start again in several months' time was minor by comparison.

By the time Giollaiosa Ó Lideadha stood up on Friday morning, it was clear he had worked as hard and long as any lawyer could be expect-ed to ensure an open-and-shut case for mistrial. He introduced a small barb in the proceedings by stating that he and Hartnett, as the ones who had attempted to introduce Oxlee's testimony, were going to seek advice from the Bar Council as to whether they could continue in a case in which they had been apparently accused by the judge, no less, of pursu-ing an "agenda… that had nothing to do with the defence" – as gross a professional calumny as any bewigged character could envisage. (The barrister in the Irish/British model is, theoretically, a legal cog who can be employed by any side of any case and who always carries out his/her duties with the utmost professionalism.)

First filling the air with the esteem in which Judge O'Donnell was held, and the hesitancy with which any lawyer seeks to criticise a judge, Ó Lideatha said that, nonetheless, there was a "substantial risk, indeed a likelihood" that an "objective observer" could doubt that justice was being seen to be done in this courtroom. He summarised the judge's sins with devastating concision: O'Donnell had prejudged a matter of fact without evidence (that is, the nebulousness and irrelevance of Oxlee's evidence); he had prejudged a matter of law without submissions (the applicability of the defence); and that he had done so, in the view of the reasonable observer, for an improper policy purpose, i.e. to uphold the right of the government to decide on matters relating to wars of other people. Ó Lideatha pointed out that a recent High Court decision in a case taken by Ed Horgan against the Shannon facility had held that it was not for the courts to interfere in matters of government policy. However, Judge O'Donnell had specifically suggested that the role of the government was proper to refer to in the interpretation of a statute in criminal law, without hearing any submissions as to the rules of statutory interpretation. "With submissions, it would have been an error. Without submissions, it raised serious concerns."

Up to the point, he said, when the defence sought to bring forward an expert witness, the only evidence as to the question of whether the action was to protect life and property etc came from the accused, a subjective source of evidence. When objective evidence was looming, the judge ruled it to be nebulous, and that it was not relevant that this action could have protected life and property in Iraq.

Then there was the nasty question of the judge's concern with the defence "agenda." Gilleoisa pointed out that the standard test for 'bias' in criminal proceedings was not even the view of the 'reasonable objective observer', but an objective person sitting in the position of the defendant. Could an objective defendant in this case reasonably perceive bias on the judge's part?

It was a long and mostly tedious day of argument, with Ó Lideatha producing a succession of law-books filled with the decisions and precedents that underlay his case for mistrial. The crowded courtroom, however, stuck with it, listening through the fuzz of detail for the real tensions and consequences beneath it. As the other defence barristers adopted Gilleoisa's case and added a few lines to it, Judge O'Donnell took the opportunity to clarify that he had not intended to suggest the lawyers had an agenda – just Ciaron O'Reilly. "I have the responsibility to ensure that the court does not lend itself to him as a political platform," he said.

This statement was enough, apparently, to cut short the supposed off-stage consultations with the Bar Council.

For the prosecution, Devally clearly hoped to keep the trial alive with O'Donnell in charge, and strongly argued against the defence submission for mistrial. For all of the loose talk about 'bias', he said, there was nothing to suggest Judge O'Donnell had any prior interest in the matter. This argument had nothing to do with bias, he said, just a possible error whereby the judge had failed to provide a hearing – it shouldn't collapse the whole trial. Maybe, just maybe, the judge had "jumped the gun," but he retained the capacity to conduct the hearing and could easily correct that error. But it could also be argued that submissions had effectively been made on the 'lawful excuse' defence already over the course of the case, and the ruling had "popped out." The judge had not shown a policy objective, and bias was a red herring. Rulings going badly for one side were not a basis for inferring bias, and there was no question here of the judge being openly hostile to the accused. (This statement drew some smirks from the audience.)

Before the end of a long day, the senior counsel for the defence landed a few more blows for the perception of bias. Hartnett said Ciaron O'Reilly's pacifism was part of his case, and his principles the basis for his actions. It was highly disturbing for the judge to say there was an improper agenda when a defendant explains to the jury the basis for his actions. O'Higgins said the basic level at which most people would judge someone to have a perceived bias is when he says "I don't want to hear what you've got to say." It was particularly unfair, he said, if this ruling "popping out" restricted the testimony of the other four defendants. And Nix went to the heart of the question about the statutory defence: if it gave too wide a scope to defendants, "it wouldn't be the first time that the lawmakers had left us a mess. If they get it wrong, the accused person is entitled to the benefit."

Judge O'Donnell said he wouldn't have time to rule on the application for discharge of the jury today – it would have to wait until Monday

morning. The weekend duly filled with speculation: what was he thinking? Who might he be consulting? Would this trial, if it continued and
ended in conviction, stand up on appeal to a higher court?

On Monday morning, March 14th, Judge O'Donnell seemed relaxed
and amiable as he began to read his ruling – and it was soon clear that
he was ruling against himself: this trial was now over. The defendants,
he said, were the most important people in a criminal trial, and it was
clear to him that there could be a perception of bias from a reasonable
defendant in this case, especially inasmuch as he had given the appear-
ance of prejudging a matter of law without submissions from counsel.
He was cool and not obviously apologetic, as though he were talking
about something that had happened entirely elsewhere. As far as he was
concerned he had not actually given a ruling on the law, he said, but just
for clarity's sake he would tell us now where he stood on it: the action
in the Shannon hangar would not, indeed, fall under the terms of the
defence because it was essentially symbolic rather than a concrete and
practical effort to protect lives and property. The giveaway, he said, was
that the defendants had "sat down on the job" to form their little circle
when they were still in a position to do further damage to the aircraft.

To protect the integrity of a future trial, he said, he was banning the
media from reporting the reason for the mistrial. He called the jury in
and sent them home with very little explanation beyond a sort of 'these
things happen'.

Although the defence was somewhat bemused by the judge's late
'ruling' on the law, those comments had absolutely no power as precedent, coming as they did at the end of a dead trial. Ciaron O'Reilly –
who back in the hangar had in fact wanted to continue bashing the plane
– was intrigued that in a nominally Christian state a judge could suggest
that saying the Rosary constituted "sitting down on the job." It didn't
show much faith in the power of prayer.

Mostly there was an air of relief that after a week of a trial that seemed
to be going so badly, the case was essentially back at square one – with

the added benefit that the defence had got to rehearse some of their arguments, and that a new judge would surely be more careful. And it was all over in plenty of time to enjoy the four-day St. Patrick's weekend. Even better, the defendants' bail conditions were quickly relaxed. In all the circumstances, including the bloody and brutal continuation of the Iraq war, it almost felt like victory. This seemed to have a particularly sunny effect on Nuin Dunlop. As defendants and supporters gathered and held hands in a big circle near the corner of the courthouse, Nuin specially thanked their secular-minded friends, and said they need not be put off by the name of their movement, 'Catholic Worker'.

"It's really full of Atheist Slackers."

Chapter 8

Try Try Again

I T WAS TO BE MORE THAN SEVEN MONTHS BEFORE ANOTHER TRIAL could get going, and with a long Irish summer in between, the anti-war movement largely dormant and little to be done in terms of legal preparation, it felt a lot like dead time. Revelations, however, about the use of Shannon for CIA rendition flights had probably improved the likely sympathies of the jury pool.

Solidarity and support were lined up again for an October 2005 re-start, and the words 'War on Trial' were excised with Orwellian precision from the environs of the case – the defendants didn't want to give the prosecution that opening again. Damien and Ciaron – who had spent part of the summer back in Brisbane with his parents – were by now a settled community of two, with occasional companions, in a house on the South Circular Road in the inner-city neighbourhood of Rialto, just around the corner from the semi-fictitious address of February 2003, where they had actually lived for some months in late 2003 and early 2004. Ciaron and Damien were working together in a homeless shelter, and maintaining a small orbit of supporters with regular liturgies, open houses and benefits. Karen and Nuin stayed with them leading up to the trial.

This time around the presiding judge was Donagh McDonagh, a more genteel character entirely than the rather down-to-earth O'Donnell, who had so honourably seen the error of his ways. There was another change of personnel below the bench. Hugh Hartnett, who had ably argued the defence in the pre-trial stage and had represented

Damien and Ciaron in the first trial, had been appointed by the Minister for Justice to investigate the death of a 14-year-old boy in police custody. The articulate if somewhat more eccentric-looking Roderick O'Hanlon had taken his place. Nix remained in place for Karen Fallon. In the row of senior defenders, Michael O'Higgins now looked positively sleek and elegant in between two rather rotund and old-fashioned bearded and moustachio'ed advocates.

The trial got off to a familiar start, but without the sort of interruptions from the judge that made the first, O'Donnell trial so entertaining and worrying. Judge McDonagh stayed largely aside, but was often called into action anyway in the first few days as long arguments about the admissibility of the 'shrine' material were replayed in the absence of the jury. McDonagh was more or less as restrictive in theory as O'Donnell – rejecting the videos, restricting the defence's capacity to talk about events that happened after February 3rd, 2003 – but apparently more accepting in the general run of the trial. And he also allowed the defence to pressure police witnesses about their failure to inspect US planes at Shannon – not only for direct violations of Irish domestic law, but for evidence that they were engaged in activities that might be in violation of the Geneva Convention, which has the status of law in Ireland.

When it came time for Ciaron O'Reilly to be cross-examined, Conor Devally, for the state, was tetchier than ever, pressing Ciaron again on his alleged eagerness to be arrested and tried and, thus, to put the "war on trial."

Ciaron insisted that he had acted with the hope that something else might have happened, even that police might have joined in the action. "If I thought there was no possibility for people to have a change of heart and resist this war, I would not have bothered to go into Shannon Airport. I may have stayed at the monastery."

"So you were hoping to change hearts?"

"Yeah, I believe it is a possibility that we are not doomed to killing children in Iraq, that we can take moral positions."

"Can I suggest, Mr O'Reilly, that this is preposterous. That [Mary] Kelly had been arrested the previous week. You broke into a hangar. You knelt down afterwards. And it was, as night follows day, you were going to be arrested. Is that right? Just say it straight."

Ciaron laughed. "Sorry to disappoint you, but no."

So what about the "war on trial"?

"As soon as I accepted the discipline of having legal representation, and that legal representation convinced me that I am innocent of this crime, I have had no intentions of putting the war on trial in this court-room…. My priority was to disable part of the US war machine, and to directly intervene in their deployment. And I think we did that."

So why not just leave the scene?

"I think we always stay and pray, and not hit and split. We do that because we are taking responsibility for our actions, and we hope that other people take responsibility for theirs and reflect on how their actions are involved in the killing of children in Iraq." Under more questioning, Ciaron added: "It could have endangered someone getting on the plane and trying to fly off with it, if it was disabled. So it is a health and safety issue too, I guess."

Devally wasn't going to let that one go lightly. Defence lawyers had spent some of the first days of the trial establishing from witnesses that the damage done to the plane was obvious and unmissable. "But you have just told this jury you stayed, in part, out of a health and safety issue… Isn't that baloney?"

"No, we were very concerned about everyone there that day. We were concerned about the lives of young US military people who would be on that plane, being shipped into a war zone. We were concerned about police officers on duty that morning. We had a general concern about everyone's health and well-being and safety."

Devally finally let Ciaron off his health and safety duties to return to the "war on trial." He read again from Ciaron's interview with Amy Goodman: "And so we are hoping to put the war on trial. We have a

website, warontrial, which will update people as the trial progresses."
Devally paused: "You did not mean that?"

"No. I think that is called 'peace on trial' now…"

"I think it is called 'peace on trial' because of our last talk, isn't that right?"

"You did make a contribution."

A small point scored, Devally sparred further with O'Reilly until he turned his attention to the meaning of a Ploughshares action.

Ciaron replied: "Ploughshares actions take their inspiration from the prophecy of Micah chapter 4 and Isaiah chapter 2, that there will come a time when people beat their swords into ploughshares, their spears into pruning hooks and study war no more. So these are non-violent attempts to enflesh that prophecy by disarming weapons of mass destruction, by disarming weapons that are aimed to kill the innocent…"

"Who devised Ploughshares actions?"

"Who devised them? Well, it is from a 3,000-year-old prophecy."

"No, no, you are talking about something recent, ploughshares actions. Who was behind them? Were you founder of them?"

Ciaron replied with his own "No no." He skipped the question of foundation, and called them "faith-based non-violent actions of disarmament. Communities come together to disarm weapons that threaten the innocent."

Devally seemed to be winding up to question whether this plane, a "liveried" 737, really constituted a weapon. "There were no weapons mounted on the plane itself… There were no bomb hatches or anything of that sort." But then Devally began to ask about O'Reilly's participation in previous Ploughshares activity, and the trial ground to another halt. The rest of the day ran out in legal argument – with Devally aiming to show that Ciaron's previous criminal Ploughshares record was relevant to the question of his alleged belief in the legality of this action and his alleged non-expectation of arrest. Eventually the day's debate was ended and a ruling postponed until the following Tuesday, so everyone could enjoy another holiday weekend.

Judge McDonagh eventually ruled in favour of Devally, but in reality the questioning that followed didn't serve the prosecution particularly well. It allowed Ciaron to talk about his experience of two previous acquittals: in Liverpool, "the women were charged with two and half million pounds of criminal damage to a Hawk jet fighter that was being sold to the Indonesian government, to be used against the people of East Timor, and that jury found those four women not guilty, and I was in the courtroom when that verdict was given. And I later attended a trial in Scotland where three women had disabled part of the Trident nuclear weapons system and the judge directed the jury to find them not guilty on the basis that Trident was indeed an illegal weapon system under international law. So that would have formed my belief that what we were doing was not guilty under local law as well as international law, and was not a crime."

Devally asked "if you've had a court experience where you were vindicated?"

"Not yet."

There was still more, and more tedious, legal argument in the jury's absence about particular lines of questioning. The tedium was relieved, however, by one of those now-rare Dublin moments that remind you of the peculiar character that still lingers around the place. In the midst of an argument about whether and when it was appropriate to interrupt a witness, Judge McDonagh said that witnesses should not "go off on a tangent." This prompted a loud interruption from a well-spoken gentleman in the court, quaintly referred to in the official transcript as "Man From The Public Gallery."

> MFTPG: Politicians normally do that, go off on a tangent.
> Judge: Can we remove that gentleman from the court.
> MFTPG: You're a fucking joke, sir.

> Judge: Place that man under arrest. I will deal with him at lunch-
> time for contempt. Put him under arrest, in the cells, I'll deal with
> him at lunchtime. I'm not going to be referred to in those tones by
> anybody.
> MFTPG: Swan eggs, please, for lunch.
> (man removed from the courtroom)

The gentleman proved to be an eccentric and barely-known cousin of one of the defence barristers – not one of the defendants, whose family and supporters had been impeccably behaved throughout their trials. He apologised and was freed just after lunchtime; it is not recorded if he was disappointed at being served something other than swans' eggs in the courthouse cells.

There was only one other telling exchange between Devally and O'Reilly, when the former suggested that the "common word" for what he had done, despite the "lofty motives that you put forward... would be 'taking the law into your own hands.'"

The phrase was as clear a summary of the prosecution case as could be imagined, and Ciaron could only try to bat it back with a flurry of his own words: "It was to disable a plane that was part of the US Navy war machine that had been killing children under the sanctions [and] was about to escalate into bombardment by the US Navy and US Air Force; to disrupt, to preserve some lives.... And it was to fulfil the law, fulfil the Constitution, to fulfil Christian teaching, to fulfil international law, and to fulfil my responsibilities under the Nuremberg principles."

Ciaron was subsequently able to discuss much further the situation in Iraq and under international law because of the unusual nature of this trial. With three barristers representing the various accused, two of them, other than his own, could "cross-examine" him – and the rules of court allow wide scope for cross-examiners, whether or not they are hostile to the witness. As a result, long stretches of questioning consisted of Nix and O'Higgins stating propositions about US perfidy in Iraq and

O'Reilly agreeing. It was hard to know if this speechifying was making much impression on the jury, however.

Just as in the first trial, the long delays and arguments were complicating the defence's plans to bring forward other witnesses. They might, as in the first trial, have to introduce an expert witness before all the defendants had testified; but that might mean, as in the first trial, that the judge would be forced to make an important ruling on the law before all the defendants had been heard. On that long Tuesday they decided, in any case, to bring on defendant Damien Moran before trying for any other witnesses.

Damien was always going to be an absolutely crucial witness, his 'disarming' youth and straightforward country charm likely to be persuasive to a jury. In the event, after the epic of Ciaron O'Reilly over two trials, Moran's spell in the stand felt almost anti-climactic – partly because the defence lawyers had their eyes on their expert witness. Damien did immediately turn on his midlands pride: "I was brought up in Banagher, County Offaly, a beautiful little town on the River Shannon." And he may have slyly appealed to anyone who had ever worked illegally in the States when he mentioned the summer when he "volunteered with a plumber" in New York. He gently referred to ex-foreign minister Brian Cowen as "a fellow county man."

The defence team was prepared to let his charm speak for itself, and to ensure his earnest and carefully well-informed goodwill shone through. His own barrister, Roderick O'Hanlon, introduced the letters Moran wrote to the Irish government before his action, letters that drew attention to the effect of sanctions in Iraq. O'Hanlon also got Moran to contradict Sergeant O'Connell's account of five shouting maniacs running into the hangar, as Moran spelled out his concern that there might be armed guards present.

Devally's cross-examination was along similar lines to what he had done with O'Reilly, concentrating on the publicity-seeking and propaganda aspect of the action and the certainty, or otherwise, of arrest and trial. In addition, perhaps remembering the cameo of Ciaron with the mattock across his lap from the first trial, Devally asked Damien to take the hammer and demonstrate how he had hammered the plane.

"Well, I don't have a plane here, so I can't really do it again."

"I'm sure you'd wish to, but we'll imagine the plane," Devally quipped.

Moran's lawyer objected. Judge McDonagh was inclined to allow the demonstration, but wondered: "Do you want him to do it with the same vigor? And what happens if that hammer flies out of his hand?"

Devally addressed Moran: "If you can avoid endangering anyone Mr Moran, and I know you wouldn't wish to do that, would you – "

"That's fair enough. I could use the inflatable hammer as a demonstration."

Devally was serious, though, and wanted to see him swing the real hammer. "You will hold up the hammer and tell us, how did you employ it?"

"Like anybody would employ a hammer," Damien replied, lifting it for more of a mime than a re-enactment. "Hold the handle and bang. Disarm part of the war machine, simple as that."

Moran was so good-natured about it that Devally soon abandoned the line of questioning, which seemed to have something to do with violence and non-violence. The rest of his cross-examination of Moran was frustrating for everyone, with Devally struggling to paint Moran as a protester, and thus the action as simply a form of protest. The barrister showed his age and social background when he cited as precedents for protest the attempts from the 1980s to stop development at Dublin's historic Viking site at Wood Quay, and from even earlier to "prevent the knocking down of Georgian properties in Hume Street." Damien pointed out that "I'm a bit young to correspond with the Wood Quay action" – though refrained from mentioning that he was also too provincial and working-class. Moran cited the IRA ceasefires and decommissioning of weapons as his prime example of the promise and possibility of peace.

Moran, like O'Reilly, finished his spell in the stand as an echo chamber for the reflections from O'Higgins and Nix about various subjects, most pointedly the dangers of attack potentially posed to Ireland because of the government's effective support for the US war effort in Iraq.

Then O'Hanlon called Dr Jean Allain, and the prosecution quickly proposed that the relevance of the witness be discussed in the absence of the jury. This was to be a key moment in the trial, the defence's first attempt to introduce evidence about the war: Allain was a senior lecturer in international law at Queen's University in Belfast. Judge McDonagh wasn't going to make Judge O'Donnell's mistake and toss him out without knowing what he had to say. Indeed, the judge decided, after legal argument, to have the lecturer testify fully in the jury's absence first, so McDonagh could assess whether the evidence was relevant and admissible in the case.

The defence's effort to introduce international law was a strategy that went beyond the straightforward 'protection of life and property' that had been the mainstay of their case to date. To show that the war was illegal might help bolster the academic legitimacy of the defendants' 'honest belief', but it also would boost a further and quite separate statutory defence: that the use of force is sometimes justified in the prevention of a crime. The defence had already been insisting, successfully, that certain offences planned and committed outside Ireland could be prosecuted in Ireland under the Geneva Convention. So Allain would help establish that there were, in fact, crimes being committed and contemplated, and that the action at Shannon was directed at preventing them.

Or he would if the judge let him testify in front of the jury. However, after Allain's no-jury 'trial run', and more long legal argument, Judge McDonagh shot him down: "Whether the war was legal or illegal has no bearing on this trial" – in part because the war had not yet started on February 3rd, 2003. Moreover, Allain had not met the accused before their action, so he could not testify that his views had any bearing on their 'honest belief'. Anyway, the judge added, the main statutory defence against the charge of criminal damage said that the accused's 'honest belief' did not actually have to be objectively 'justified' – so evidence that justified those beliefs was immaterial.

With a deep breath at seeing one plank of the defence removed, the lawyers called Geoffrey Oxlee – the prospect of whose testimony had been enough to send Judge O'Donnell spluttering toward mistrial seven months previously. The defence team immediately offered to have Oxlee heard in the jury's absence. The judge this time around seemed slightly puzzled as to why this witness was even questionable. Giollaiosa Ó Lideadha explained the reason to hear Oxlee: "For the purpose of establishing for the jury that… a supply vehicle… would be regarded as a legitimate target for defence forces to take against an offensive force… to reduce the effectiveness of the attacking force."

"I don't see any great controversy about that," McDonagh said, to the bemusement of everyone who had suffered through the first trial.

Oxlee, nevertheless, first gave his testimony in the jury's absence. A former Group Captain in the Royal Air Force, where he served for 33 years, he was an acknowledged and experienced expert on military analysis, with an OBE from "Her Majesty the Queen." He was so much an obvious paragon of the British military establishment that you could see the defendants squirming at his apparent support, and the implication that their action could be viewed in terms of military tactics. Oxlee was even an honorary member of the US Navy after having served as a place-kicker on a Navy football team.

But when he told O'Higgins that taking one supply plane out of circulation "would have had an influence," his usefulness could hardly have been clearer.

When his brief evidence finished, McDonagh scolded the prosecution: "You should keep your objections for the crucial evidence… I can see no objection to this evidence." Oxlee duly repeated his testimony with the jury present – Devally reduced to making the point that as of

February 3rd, 2003, the only "defensive force" that might have wanted to attack a US asset would be working for Saddam Hussein.

Before Oxlee stepped down, O'Higgins teased one last useful point out of him: military operations that might strictly be regarded as futile are nonetheless sometimes attempted because of their potential capacity to inspire others and to set off a positive chain reaction, including an effect on how people think. The old *Beyond the Fringe* comedy sketch in which wartime officers seek a volunteer for a "futile gesture" told an essential truth, Oxlee said. The British, he added, "are very good at celebrating honourable failures, and there have been many."

O'Higgins continued: "When [the US and British governments] heard that a plane had been disabled, married with a clarion call for other people to join in this activity, that is something that could cause them concern?"

"And undoubtedly it did."

"And if they reached the… tipping point where there was mass involvement inspired by this act that could cause very serious difficulties?"

"Well, if could if it had happened."

"…. Sometimes the inspiration works, and sometimes it doesn't. Isn't that so?"

It was a moment of genuine poignancy, recalling all that had happened to Iraq in the intervening two-and-a-half years. After a lunch break in which the spectators shared their goosebumps, there was to be more emotional testimony: the defence called former US Marine platoon sergeant Jimmy Massey, an honest and brave Southerner who had been speaking emotionally at public events running alongside the trial.

Massey arrived in Iraq in January 2003 near the end of his 12 years of service. Again, after argument, he was heard in the absence of the jury, testifying about the importance of Shannon Airport in the military logistics chain – "beans, bullets and band-aids" – and about the intelligence briefings he received telling him that any Iraqi was to be regarded as "a potential terrorist or target…. Shoot first, ask questions later." Judge McDonagh gave him the go-ahead to proceed in the jury's presence, where he added that with a "carte blanche to kill" he had seen the killing of "30-plus innocent civilians" between March and May 2003.

It had been a remarkable day in court, beginning with the rejection of Allain but including potentially powerful evidence from Oxlee and Massey. Now, with these time-limited 'experts' disposed of, we were ready to return to the witnesses who had no choice but to be present: the defendants. Karen Fallon climbed into the stand. She was quiet – "sweet Scottish tones," Nix said – but direct and distinctly unflaky. Why did she do it?

"Well, primarily to stop them killing people, you know, and destroying the hospitals and waterworks. It's okay for us here, you know, nobody is going over to bomb us every day. Primarily just to try and stop them doing it."

But the invasion hadn't happened yet, right?

"The official invasion, as they call it the shock and awe thing, hadn't taken place. But the war was still happening. It never really stopped." She described seeing the build-up to the new phase of war in Faslane, and how she tried to make a difference at Shannon: "They say it is a logistics plane, but you cannot run a war without your everyday things, like toilet roll…. If it saved one life, then it is worth it."

Devally pressed her, as he had done O'Reilly and Moran, on the symbolic and publicity-seeking elements of the action, the shrine, the slogans. Why had she carried the inflatable hammer?

"Well, you see I was kind of frightened at the time… and I kind of thought it would be pretty hard to shoot someone if they had a green, white and gold hammer in their hands…. We went in that hangar thinking we could have been shot. Now you are turning it into some sort of smutty little thing for the newspapers, and it is just not true."

Devally sparred with her for several minutes over the word 'protest'. Karen eventually replied: "This action was not a protest. This action was a small attempt, sure, but an attempt to stop them killing people."

Then it was Deirdre Clancy's turn. She was quiet too, but strong and clear, if less colourful and direct than Karen. The pattern of challenging the defendants was so clear by now that Devally left it to his junior counsel to cross-examine Deirdre, and predictably they skirmished around the concept of 'protest' until there was no time left in the day. The trial resumed with Clancy in the box on the Thursday morning, November 3rd, 2005, when she gave her view of the Catholic Worker: "I wouldn't say that all Catholic Workers have a strong relationship with the institutional church – some do, and some don't. There are different degrees of involvement in Catholicism as an institution, but there are people of all creeds involved in the Catholic Worker – there are atheists, there are Buddhists, it is a very diverse movement." The prosecutor then chose to press her about her religious beliefs, and why she and other defendants "affirmed" that their testimony would be truthful rather than swearing on the Bible – an intrusive and unproductive line of questioning, it appeared, since Deirdre's faith and sincerity were so clearly evident. So had she expected to be arrested?

"I think the Ploughshares tradition contains a hope… that those in authority would join in the action. It may seem naïve, but in fact without that hope Ploughshares would be meaningless. But common sense would dictate that in the climate at the time, we would be arrested. I knew that was a probability."

In one exchange Deirdre's clarity, moral and otherwise, might have unwittingly weakened the defence case, especially in light of the impact of Oxlee's testimony, during which their own lawyers had painted the accused as near-commandos. How, the prosecutor wondered, could they both be inviting others to join in and at the same sneaking around at night, "working under cover, so to speak?"

"I don't think we were under cover," Deirdre replied. "I think we would have been quite visible when we were, for instance... outside the hangar when the shrine was being constructed. We were not dressed in black clothes with balaclavas, we were dressed normally, and to say we were under cover makes it sound like something rather sinister. I think that is misleading."

The prosecutor saw his opening: "Right, let's accept then I'm wrong about that, and that rather you were doing this in a way which made it all the more inevitable that you were going to be found out, and arrested." Indeed.

It is striking when observing these trials that for all the care and precision taken over words and statutes and certain details of the case, other apparently simple matters remain inexplicably vague. In the trials of the Pitstop Ploughshares, for example, no one on either side seemed willing or able to pin down the date of the Féile Bríde conference in Kildare. Since every Irish person knows that St Bridget's Day falls on February 1st, some accuracy on this matter was actually material to the case. How could the defendants have attended the festival, returned to Dublin, gone for several days on retreat to Glenstal and then cased Shannon to prepare for their action, which took place in the wee hours of February 3rd?

It's easy when you know the 2003 conference took place mainly on Saturday, January 25th, but thoroughly inexplicable otherwise. As Nuin Dunlop took the stand for the first time that Thursday morning, her own senior counsel, Michael O'Higgins, illustrated the ignorance: "There has been evidence in the case that you met up, perhaps around the 29th of January, or thereabouts, for the Saint Brigid's commemoration mass." And so any juror trying to do the math in her head was getting misleading information even from this most reputable of sources.

"Very American" is rarely a compliment in Ireland, but it might have been on this day. Nuin, the American defendant, was the most frankly spiritual and perhaps the most obviously deliberate and deliberative in her testimony. The shrine, she said carefully, was "a prayer." She admitted it was "a fairly intangible thing to say" but "that is what it was." Her blue eyes opened wide as she recalled entering the hangar: "I initially paused for quite a while, because I was so shocked to actually see a US Navy war-plane here in Ireland. I literally could not believe my eyes, and I paused, and just stared, I had heard that there were war-planes here, and I knew this war in Iraq was to take place, but to actually see a plane with my own eyes was such a surprise that I literally couldn't move."

It was a far cry from Sergeant O'Connell's tale of screaming invaders, and you could see the jury liked it. So why did she do this action?

"There were several reasons, four reasons actually. I would say the words responsibility, solidarity, urgency and prayer – and please if I could explain?" The whole courtroom willed her to explain. "Responsibility to me means literally the ability to respond: I'm not an Iraqi person standing under the threat of bombardment, I'm not an economic conscript in the US military, I am a person who had an ability to respond to what I saw was going to be the killing of innocent people, and so I had the ability to respond, I did respond. Secondly, solidarity: solidarity to me is 'being with,' it is a presence with people who are suffering in some way, and I saw the Iraqi people as very much suffering under psychological threat of potential full-on war; and I wanted to say to those people in Iraq, you are seen, you are heard, and you are not alone in this; so that is solidarity, it is 'being with,' even from a slight distance. Urgency: I had a sense that war was imminent, that bombs were going to be crashing down on people in the very near future, and that people's lives in Iraq were at risk, and action needed to be taken to protect the people and the land of Iraq. And prayer: I had a sense through prayer that I needed to participate in this particular action at Shannon."

Sure, it was a well thought-out piece of speech-making, but it was a beautiful one too, and from this striking woman, a dark-haired mix of Irish and Native American, it blew like a breeze of truth through the courtroom. When Devally tried to probe her on why, if she was living in

Scotland, she chose to come to Ireland to act, Nuin gave another answer, this time clearly unrehearsed, that had heads nodding and eyes filling up.

"Yes, it is a question I have thought a lot about. I was in the area at the time, and I have a great deal of respect for Ireland, I always have. I think a lot of Americans – I think especially Americans of Irish descent, and I am partly of Irish descent – we grew up with all sorts of notions about Ireland being – you know, rightly or wrongly – about Ireland being a peaceful country. I can remember having conversations with people in the States who were so proud of their Irish ancestry. I would ask: why are you so proud of a thing like an ancestry?... It is a country of peace, a neutral country, a country that stands up to people oppressing the innocent all over the world, and Irish people in solidarity with people in some of the poorest countries on earth for centuries.... This is just part of the myth, you could say, that Irish-Americans grew up with.... When I did visit here and I heard about Shannon, I could not believe what was going on. I knew, as a US citizen, that it was my own country's government that was allowing these war-planes to go through your country, and there is a part of me that just felt very sorry for that.... I wanted to apologise to the people in this country for that happening. I will apologise right now, for my country using your country in such a way." She looked at the jury. "I'm sorry, I'm truly sorry that is happening."

Under Devally's usual "this was just a protest" line of questioning, Nuin came up with an apparently spontaneous metaphor: "If you can imagine the people of Iraq, or a large group of civilians in Iraq, standing with a chain wrapped around them – let's say the chain is rusty, and has barbed wire on it, and it is being pulled tighter and tighter until they are being crushed by this chain. And at Shannon Airport, because of my country's use of that airport, is a signature link in this chain – and if that link can be broken, then the chain itself might fall apart, and then people would live."

One good American deserves another, and the defence called Kathy Kelly. This call, of course, set off another long argument in the jury's absence. In the course of it, Judge McDonagh made a comment that would have been entirely normal in the context of a political argument, but seemed strange from a judge in a criminal trial: "I have one problem with the language that has been used throughout this case and the slant that has been put throughout this case, that this was a war that was being perpetrated on the Iraqi people, without ever a mention from anybody of what had been perpetrated on the Iraqi people by their own leaders.... It is so one-sided, the approach to this, that I am actually concerned."

Brendan Nix was concerned about the judge's concern: "The prosecution is here to take care of their side, the defence is here to take care of ours. You're the man in the middle and you have no concern except to show a fair trial, for the five people, not for the American Army or George W. Bush or Tony Blair. There are five people on trial here, they are your only concerns."

McDonagh ruled that Kelly could testify, but only about what she said at Féile Bríde in 2003. "That is going to require an element of honour, which I think has pervaded this case," he said. In the end, Kelly's testimony was brief, to the point, and necessarily emotive, just as her talk in 2003 had been. For example, she said, "I told them that in 1998 I myself had gone into the obstetrics hospital... and all of the windows had been blown out by a bombing and I remember being with mothers in that obstetrics ward, so you could understand why people were in great fear." She spoke of the photographs that had ended up in the shrine, and of what they said about the ongoing nature of the war against the Iraqi people.

Most extraordinarily, she was followed into the witness box by Denis Halliday without so much as a break, let alone a long legal argument. In a welter of further confusion about dates, he revealed to the surprise of most people, including the prosecution, that he had not in fact spoken in Kildare at the 2003 festival, but had been heard by the five at the

February 1st rally at Shannon Airport. Halliday was also the star-turn in John Pilger's *Paying the Price* documentary, which had been left at the shrine, and he got a chance to talk about his role in that. He was business-like, the alternative to Kelly's more emotional tone. Were 5,000 Iraqi children a month really dying from sanctions?

"The figure varies. In the summer months when the climate is more benign the figures would often drop to two or three thousand per month. In the winter months, and Iraq does have a very severe winter, the death rate increased. Because children were dying of diarrhoea, dysentery, a cold would become bronchitis and pneumonia because they didn't have drugs to stop it. It's not sophisticated stuff, this is very simple."

And that, finally, on the Thursday afternoon of the second week, was the end of evidence in the trial. Judge McDonagh appeared pleased: "Very good, well gentlemen, I take it you will need some time for speeches?"

Devally replied first. "There is an issue that will have to be ventilated before your lordship."

"Ah."

"Which I have signalled – "

"How hopeful of me that we could move on."

Everyone agreed it would be best to send the jury home for the weekend, because the court was going to first have to deal with the thorny question of the 'lawful excuse' defence. As Devally put it: "The purpose of the application that I bring now is to apply that your lordship deprive the jury of consideration of the defence; in other words, that it does not go to the jury." He said he was going to use (mostly British) case law to show that while "the consideration of the honest belief is held to be a subjective test, but other features to the defence are objective, and not alone objective, but objective and capable and in fact necessary to be looked at by the judge. And it being a matter of law as to whether the facts of that particular case are as such to allow for the defence at all." Matters of law, it seems, are for judges to determine; only matters of fact can be left to the jury to decide.

The legal debate that Friday was exhaustive and exhausting, trying the patience of even the growing band of amateur lawyers among the five's support. The defence team seemed to do a good job of blowing holes in the state's application, but it was hard to be sure. In pre-trial, Judge Mathews had agreed with the defence after a more truncated version of this argument; in the first trial Judge O'Donnell had appeared to plump for the prosecution after very little argument at all; Judge Carroll Moran had shot down the defence in both of Mary Kelly's trials. What would Judge McDonagh do?

In the absence of the jury on Monday morning, soon after 10.30am, it was quickly apparent that he was unpersuaded by the defence case. While everyone in court accepted that the accused had acted with an honest belief – thus passing the so-called 'subjective test' – the 'objective' question of lawful excuse was essentially a matter of interpreting the law, and thus a question for the judge to decide, he said.

The key testimony on the question, he said, was Geoffrey Oxlee's – and that had failed to establish that the action at Shannon had specifically protected any particular life or property. Moreover, the five had not done enough damage to avail of the defence: perhaps, one wondered, if they had roamed the airport wrecking all the US equipment they could find…

This was, essentially, Judge O'Donnell's quasi-decision revisited, right down to the word "nebulous" – though McDonagh did not actually accuse the defendants of sitting down on the job. The connection between the action and the alleged protection was "too tenuous, nebulous and remote when viewed objectively," the judge said. He was granting the state application that the defence be withheld from the jury. As a small mercy, the judge said he would not actually direct the jury to bring in a guilty verdict, he simply would not permit them to deliberate with the help of the 'lawful excuse' defence.

And, oh yes, the other defence that had been raised, that the action could be justified by the statute that permits the use of force to prevent a crime? That didn't really apply either, on obscure technical grounds.

The defence team were, in the Irish terminology, gobsmacked. The three senior defence counsel were expected to make closing speeches today, and the judge's comprehensive decision had thrown them back into the realm of emotional appeals rather than the legal argument they had planned. After a short recess, they shot back: let us bring Oxlee to the witness stand again so we can plug the gaps and make the connection less tenuous. (The defence had previously insisted that the statutory defence didn't actually require definite specificity as to the life- and property-saving effect of the action.) The debate on this application, opposed by the prosecution, occasionally bordered on emotional. The judge said he would give his decision after the lunch break.

Meanwhile, however, from the time of the first recess after McDonagh's decision, the defendants were hearing from their lawyers about a 'nuclear option' – an extraordinary phrase in the circumstances, but it neatly described the likely effect of the weapon they had found in their arsenal. O'Higgins rose just before the break and dropped a hint: "A matter has been brought to our attention this morning and there may be an issue arising afterwards which will affect the course of the trial. I am awaiting further instructions."

"I await with bated breath," the judge replied, with his usual charm.

Over lunchtime the defendants and their lawyers talked through their options. The team had, apparently in the last couple of days, acquired a piece of information, gossip really, that would almost certainly pull the plug on this trial. The judge's decision had gone so comprehensively against them that there was scarcely any risk in ending this second trial and hoping for third time lucky. The decision was simple.

Ciaron and Damien's senior counsel, Roderick O'Hanlon, stood up after lunch, in the jury's absence, and explained: the defence understood that Judge McDonagh had attended George W. Bush's inauguration in

2001 and had indeed been invited back to Washington for the repeat in 2005. If this were the case, O'Hanlon said, he might be asked to disqualify himself. Jaws hung slack around the courtroom.

"At this point," the Indymedia reporter eloquently put it, "Judge McDonagh laughed aloud, and alone."

O'Higgins proceeded to put a question to the judge. According to the details given to the defence, McDonagh, back in his days as a barrister, had attended an event in Houston, Texas, in the mid-1990s and been photographed with then-governor Bush. He had attended the 2001 presidential inauguration and been invited back for the second Inauguration by House of Representatives majority leader Tom DeLay. He had been unable to attend in 2005 because of a schedule conflict. McDonagh confirmed that the information was basically correct, though he also said it was "half right."

The judge was evidently unamused, and said his personal life was not a matter for this court. But he was cornered, and the defence team drove home their advantage with a polite but firm application that he discharge the jury, not because he had shown any bias – God no! – but because of the potential for a 'perception of bias' arising from his connection to a man whose character and military policy loomed over this whole case. Any juror with such a connection to Bush would surely be disqualified, they said.

McDonagh called a short recess and asked the lawyers to meet him in his chambers. The barristers instead hung around the courtroom, Nix nipping out for a puff on his pipe, while the judge stewed alone. Just after 3pm Judge McDonagh was back, looking flushed with anger. He called in the jury and told them that the trial was over. He gave them no explanation, adjourned the case and flew from the room. He hadn't even remembered to bar media reporting of the reason for the trial collapse, and reporters ran out to write the embarrassing stories. But the defence had done him a favour: if his connection to Bush had been revealed in an appeal to a higher court against an eventual conviction, it would have surely have been more damaging.

It was Monday, November 7th, 2005, nearly three years since the action at Shannon. Twice in eight months the Pitstop Ploughshares had seen trials collapse because a judge had permitted a 'perception of bias' against them to enter the courtroom. Even Devally was turning up his eyes in despair and sympathy when he encountered the defendants. Supporters raised their voices for the charges to be dropped. What would it take for the Shannon Five to get a fair hearing?

Chapter 9

Conscience of the Community

I
T WAS ANOTHER EIGHT MONTHS UNTIL THE DATE FOR THE NEXT
trial rolled around. For the defendants it was in some ways a more
eventful period than the previous delay. Four of the five of them took
advantage of much-relaxed bail conditions (well, they had shown up for
trial twice already) to leave the country for most of the waiting time:
Nuin to travel, Karen home to Scotland, Damien to the new home he
was hoping to make in Poland and Ciaron back to Australia. Ciaron
managed to raise Australian media interest in the case, especially after
he appeared on TV and quoted Dorothy Day: "The church is a whore,
but she's my mother." But the accused and their case were virtually invis-
ible in Ireland for the first half of 2006.

By the time the third trial started on July 10th, 2006, the Irish media
had apparently decided it didn't much care. Sure, the inflatable hammer
had made cute headlines twice before, but this looked an awful lot like
a repeat. The fact that, on previous evidence, it was predictable that testimony would get interrupted for lots of legal argument in the absence
of the jury rendered it still less attractive: it was no good having a paid
reporter sitting in a courtroom if a large part of the proceedings couldn't
actually be reported. Anyway, it was summertime, and despite the shortage of good weather in Ireland the Irish people tend to give themselves
the longest possible time to enjoy whatever sun and heat does manifest
itself. Newspapers tend to get light, in every sense of the word.

Apart from the novelty of summer outdoors, the trial in the Dublin
Circuit Court did feel like *déjà vu*. Even the joys of international soli-

darity and the daily walk from O'Connell Street seemed a little tired: no 'objective observer' could possibly have concluded that there was a substantial body of active support here. In the courtroom, there were slight personnel changes: John O'Kelly, the oldest of the advocates in this case, took over as Damien and Ciaron's senior counsel, and of course there was a new judge, Miriam Reynolds, youngish-looking for a judge, fastidious and rather nerdy. After a momentary panic when supporters recalled that former Fianna Fail prime minister Albert Reynolds had a daughter called Miriam who had studied law – phew, no, this wasn't her – no one could give any reason for either optimism or pessimism about the latest lady m'lord.

It seemed hard to remember that for the jurors this was all brand new. The prosecution case was familiar, and the defendants too covered mostly old ground. Damien was pressed on his March 2003 statement that he looked forward to going to a trial before a jury, the conscience of the community. Karen broke into tears as she recalled building the shrine. Nuin sparred with the prosecutor the same as before, but she joked afterward that she could see a perverse bond between them – she said that if there were another mistrial she and Devally would commit hara-kiri on the courtroom floor in a final embrace. On the other hand, war in the Middle East was a living reality on daily television: the atmosphere was heightened from the third day of the trial by the outbreak of by Israel's invasion of Lebanon.

Geoffrey Oxlee gave his evidence to the jury despite the state's objections – standing up in the box this time as his arthritic hip bothered him: his almost Pythonesque military bearing was only enhanced as a result. Judge Reynolds, however, decided to hear Kathy Kelly, Denis Halliday, Jimmy Massey and Dr Jean Allain in the absence of the jury to test their relevance and admissibility. The jury got a long weekend: they were out of the courtroom from the afternoon of Thursday, July 13th to late on Monday, July 17th while these witnesses were heard and argued about. Unlike Judge McDonagh in the second trial, who refused only Allain of that foursome, Reynolds decided that both Halliday and Massey were impermissible, but allowed the international law expert – while withholding her ruling on whether 'prevention of a crime' could be a defence in this case. Apart from heightening the sense of randomness that now hung over the whole process, in strict terms of the scorecard, this looked worse than McDonagh; but the defence team seemed especially pleased to get Allain in front of the jury. Even if they couldn't ultimately use the 'prevent a crime' defence, if the jury was to hear that the consensus among legal experts was that the war in Iraq was illegal, they might form the view that the accused acted reasonably in an attempt to hamper the war.

Allain's testimony was short and to the point. Kathy Kelly, who had been instructed by the judge to confine herself to her own experience, was longer, typically fleshing out her answers with human stories as well as statistics. Brendan Nix, questioning her, strained to get some of Denis Halliday's story into evidence despite Halliday having been barred by the judge. Was she aware of Denis Halliday's resignation from the UN? Kelly replied that she was.

Judge Reynolds, who had already interrupted a number of witnesses, broke in to ask how Kelly knew this information. If it was simply as a result of it being in the public record, it was not relevant here. Kathy Kelly said she knew Denis Halliday and had spoken with him many times. Judge Reynolds repeated her question: how had Kelly had been made aware of Mr Halliday's resignation?

Nix, miming impatience and seeing his chance, pointed towards a man on the public benches. He asked Kelly if she could identify the bearded man in the salmon-pink shirt as Denis Halliday. Kelly did so. The jury craned forward to have a look at this now-legendary figure, and perhaps to wonder why this was the only glimpse they were getting of him.

There were more tetchy exchanges as O'Higgins tried to question Kelly, with Judge Reynolds warning that she did not expect to have to admonish counsel from the bench like children, and expected them to behave themselves. (There was no doubt that the gender dynamic – most of the jury were also women – created a different effect here from in the previous trials, when at times all the senior counsel seemed to throw their weight around in front of a 'mere' Circuit Court judge.)

Wednesday, July 19th, its eighth day, was to be the crunch day in this trial, with all the well-rehearsed arguments about the law played out again in the absence of the jury. Judge Joseph Mathews had opened space for 'lawful excuse' in the pre-trial process way back in 2003. In the two aborted trials over the previous 16 months the space had been closed down again. Judge Reynolds had been a real stickler so far in this trial, but had never been anything other than fair and meticulous. If she ruled against the defence, the trial was highly likely to run on to a conclusion anyway, and the defendants were going to have a hell of a fight to avoid conviction.

Off-stage, as it were, Ciaron was arguing within the group that if Judge Reynolds ruled against them, it would be time to abandon their highly legalistic strategy and fight the case politically and emotionally, in the American Plowshares tradition. He had always believed that the defendants should at least partly represent themselves: barristers, he said again, are professionally obliged to get you off at all costs, despite the theology or the politics. Ciaron said at least Deirdre and Damien, as the 'native' Irish defendants, should be prepared to 'fire' their barristers in that event so they could make their closing speeches for themselves, straight to a Dublin jury's heart. Deirdre, who was even paler and thinner than usual at that point, getting quite visibly ill, could hardly have relished that prospect. The legal team was also not impressed by the suggestion, and Gilleoisa convinced the rest of the group that they should be prepared to press on and be represented by counsel no matter what happened. He told the five to trust that their moral values as well as legal rights would be reflected in the barristers' closing speeches.

Ciaron, meanwhile, scheduled a 'prison support workshop' where supporters could plan on how they were going to provide solidarity for the five after they were sent to prison and use their jailing for anti-war purposes. Reynolds, it was felt, would probably remand them in custody immediately if they were convicted, even while she considered their sentences, so bags were being packed. Officers from Mountjoy women's prison had been seen waiting around the court.

Before a verdict could even be deliberated, however, there were two points for Judge Reynolds to rule on. The defence team knew they had a struggle to convince the judge to let the jury consider Section 18 of the Non-Fatal Offences Against the Person Act 1997, essentially the 'prevention of a crime' defence. Sure enough, she shot that down: the defence could apply, she said, only to the offences in that act, which didn't include criminal damage.

Section 21 of the same act, however, clearly amended Section 6 of the Criminal Damage Act 1991. And what it told the legal reader was that a defendant could be deemed to have a lawful excuse to damage property in the "honest belief" that "it was in order to protect himself or another or property belonging to himself or another ... and the act or acts alleged to constitute the offence were reasonable in the circumstances as he believed them to be." Thanks to the 1997 amendment, the threat from which someone or something was being protected need not be 'immediate.' The honest belief was subjective, the reasonableness (at least to some degree) objective. No one was really arguing with the defendants' honest belief, but could a reasonable person in their position have drawn the same conclusions about a threat to life and property and the proper means to thwart that threat?

Judge Reynolds didn't have to answer that question, just to decide by interpreting the law if a jury should be allowed to consider it. She didn't seem to find the decision terribly challenging: the reasonableness of the action, she said, was a question of fact, not a matter of interpreting the law – putting it in the purview of the jury rather than of the judge. Since the defendants' honesty was not in question, she said that in this case only the reasonableness of the belief, the objective test, was at issue, and that issue was so tied up with the facts of the case as presented in evidence that she could not deprive the jury of its duty to adjudicate on it.

Some of the spectators, hearing another pair of rulings that seemed to be half-bad, half-good, weren't sure what to think. The defendants, knowing that the second decision was much more crucial than the first, were pleased. Their lawyers, fully cognisant of what they had just achieved, looked like they could weep for joy. Whatever the outcome of the case, they had already made legal history by successfully arguing the applicability of this defence. Now they would be able to make closing statements that utilized it, and could count on the judge ruling it in with her own charge to the jury. Conor Devally, the prosecutor, looked nonplussed, and said he would need some time to consider how to make a closing statement that, in effect, told the jury that while the defence could apply in theory, it didn't really, according to the facts of this case.

By the time he stood up the following morning to make the final case for conviction, Devally recognized he had another challenge. Even if he had been a war-supporter – and he decidedly wasn't – there was clearly no point in trying to buck the anti-war mood that was long latent in Irish society and had filled Court 23 for nearly two weeks. He had seen the jurors nodding in agreement at Nuin Dunlop, Kathy Kelly and others. He had to allow them to go on feeling this way, even admiring the defendants, while at the same time encouraging them to stand for the integrity of a set of laws that could not, surely, allow people to take actions like the one at Shannon.

He was further hampered by the fact that in opening the case 10 days earlier, he had forgotten to give the little lecture about 'presumption of innocence;' instead the judge had given it a few days later, but good legal manners said he had better revisit that issue, and remind the jury from the start that it was up to the prosecution to prove each element of the case and to negate every element of the defence.

So Devally opened his speech with as gracious an apology as he could muster. His omission, he said, probably happened because of the unusual nature of this case, with defendants pleading not-guilty but offering no dispute about the main facts. "None of the five is saying 'I wasn't there' and none of them is saying 'I didn't know what I was doing.'"

He continued: "The operations man at Shannon Airport gave evidence that no one had permission to enter there other than the Garda and the U.S. military and other such authorized persons. This is not in dispute. The plane belonged to the U.S. Navy. This is not in dispute. All that is left re this section of the charge is the question of lawful excuse. Do you accept from the evidence volunteered by the accused that they had lawful excuse? All the other elements of a crime are there."

Devally quoted from the defence as spelled out in the pre-amended Criminal Damage Act 1991, complete with the word "immediate."

He sympathised with the defendants for their long wait, "living in a black hole," and added, "I thought I would never be giving this presentation in court!" But the process had started, he said, with their actions at Shannon Airport.

The prosecution, he said, represents the office of the Director of Public Prosecutions on behalf of the people of Ireland. "I have no axe to grind for the United States or George W. Bush. I'm acting for the DPP to prosecute a criminal act."

As for the accused: "Their conscience is not on trial. Their morals are not on trial. We're not here to condemn their view. Were their acts reasonable?... They are sincere. This is not a sham. But were they trying to do something more nebulous, something symbolic, something that was political? Have we not heard this even from their own mouths?"

He flashed his own credentials: "On February 15th, 2003, people marched to avert war. I walked in a march, all those who marched were protesting in order to save lives, to avert war."

Ciaron O'Reilly, he said, had given all sorts of reasons for action that were not simply about protecting lives and property. "He said it was a call to others to carry out non-violent resistance to war. He believed Shannon could become a terrorist target. He wanted people to seriously reflect on non-violent action. He was putting out a call to others to take non-violent action. He described the Catholic Worker commitment to face responsibility. This is not a lawful excuse....

"You may feel the action of the defendants was a call to arms to raise the conscience of the Irish people concerning what was happening in Iraq.... But this is a democracy. We have a police, we have elected representatives. Our democracy, like all democracies, may be imperfect – the essence of a democracy is imperfection. History is littered with efforts to create a perfect state. Efforts to create perfect societies have led to fascism and totalitarianism....Ciaron O'Reilly broke the door because he said it was an emergency. Yet they went on a retreat for four days....

"They took the law into their own hands.

"We live in a country that has law, a system, a vote, a voice. They said that's not good enough, we will do something more. They had no lawful excuse. No emergency....

"All five were raising public opinion to stop others from going to war. This is laudable.... It is not a lawful excuse....

"What they did was very brave, hats off to them. They did what they did, they knew it was criminal. It was a conscience-raising exercise. And they looked forward to this trial. You must decide whether what they did falls on the wrong side of the line. Democracy does not allow people to take the law into their own hands."

Devally finished up by dismissing two of the key defence experts. The evidence of Dr Jean Allain that the war was an international crime "should not be a consideration" – as the judge had more or less ultimately decided. As for Geoffrey Oxlee, the idea that attacking a supply plane might be a legitimate war aim was irrelevant: the jury should remember that the defendants were not Iraqi insurgents, and that at any rate the "possibility" that they had an effect down the line was in the realm of chaos theory.

Next up was Karen Fallon's senior barrister, Brendan Nix. Devally had called him "the last of the great orators", and it was soon apparent why. A sonorous crescendo of words, an almost free-associative mix of current affairs and moral philosophy, with just a little law thrown in, his closing speech triggered immediate goosebumps and, by the end, tears around the courtroom.

After opening with some words about parables and parallels, Nix declared like a preacher: "Mr Devally has said the action of these defendants was a political act. I'll tell you of someone who made a great political speech, the greatest political speech of all time and that's Jesus Christ. And the name of the political speech he made was 'The Sermon on the Mount'. You'll find it in Matthew chapter 5, verses 3 to 10. This is what it says: 'Blessed are the poor in spirit: for theirs is the kingdom of heaven. Blessed are the meek: for they shall possess the land. Blessed are they who mourn: for they shall be comforted. Blessed are they that hunger and thirst after justice: for they shall have their fill. Blessed are the merciful: for they shall obtain mercy. Blessed are the peacemakers: for they shall be called the children of God. Blessed are they that suffer persecution for justice sake, for theirs is the kingdom of heaven.'

"These are the words of Our Lord and Saviour Jesus Christ, and Jesus is one of the greatest pacifists that ever lived on this earth.

"Now Lebanon is burning. Today children swimming in a pool were bombed. A swimming pool is now filled with burning children. This is war. People in Gaza are suffering and children dying.

"Now, I ask you: Would you take an axe to destroy an Israeli plane or a Hizbullah rocket? We may ask 'What is good?' Forrest Gump's mother has the answer: 'Good is as good does.'

"Today there are a lot of a la carte Catholics. They go to the sacraments for weddings and baptisms. The children make their first Communion. They go to confession now and then. They pick and choose. The trouble is, these people here" – he swung his fingers around to the defendants behind him – "believe what they are saying. To work in a wet hostel – that's not easy.

"The Commandments can all be summed up in one maxim: Love God and your neighbour. If everyone followed this commandment there would be no war....

"You have been given evidence of an uncontested statistic: more than 500,000 children under five years of age killed by the sanctions in Iraq. If one thousand children had been so killed in Ireland, there would be outrage. There's another statistic uncontested: 1.5 million people died in Iraq because of the UN sanctions. That's a quarter of the number who were killed in the Holocaust. Now I want to ask you: If you knew and cared, would you do something?

"Christ went to Gethsemane. These five went to Glenstal....

"What would rise you to action? If a child's plastic ball rolled into the street and the child ran after it, would you leave it to the Garda to go after the child?

"Or if a child's beach ball went into the water, and the child went into the water and risked drowning, would you leave it to the life-guards?...

"Iraqis have died. And these people here are such believers and have such honestly held beliefs that for them there are no strangers....

"I was in a park today and two children were being followed by a duck. There was the sound of children playing in the yard close by – children playing in a yard, and a band was playing, and there was no drunkenness. A sound of universal happiness is the sound of children playing.

"At that same time, Lebanon and Hizbullah were hammering the shite – " He stopped, as sobs could be heard. "And I asked myself, 'What right have I to be happy?'

"Where is our shared humanity? If anyone of us is cut, do we not bleed?"

There was some more in this extraordinary vein. Ciaron need not have worried, it seemed, about his politics and theology being represented.

John O'Kelly, specifically representing Ciaron and Damien, was next on his feet to speak to the jury, with a tough act to follow. Sensibly, he chose the straightforward "three principles to guide you in the jury room" approach. These were the presumption of innocence, the lawful-excuse defence itself, and "beyond reasonable doubt."

He suggested Devally had protested too much on the presumption of innocence, and neglected "beyond reasonable doubt." Having outlined its importance, the prosecutor had then "with his imaginary line and certain movements of his hands" given the impression that the jury had to weigh up probabilities. "This is nothing to do with it. The standard is beyond reasonable doubt. It's not a question of there being two sides and 'Do you prefer this or that?'

"We're here to try defendants in relation to a particular criminal offence, not to examine a continuum of options for action. The burden is on the prosecution to prove every element of the alleged offence, beyond reasonable doubt."

As for the lawful excuse: "the accused person does not have to prove it, but prosecution must convince you, also beyond reasonable doubt, that a lawful excuse does *not* apply."

O'Kelly analytically explained that the defence being employed couldn't be regarded as a licence to kill. The statute "is strictly talking about damage to property, not to life. It's not as if the law is saying that it would be alright to put a bomb under a plane to prevent it from going to Iraq, as this would itself endanger life."

He pointed out too that an immediate danger was not a requirement for the statutory defence, despite what Devally had said. In any case, the 5,000 miles to Iraq might have been a long distance many years ago. "Now we can go that distance in four hours."

Most amusingly, O'Kelly seemed to scold Devally for the latter's praise of the defendants. "Towards the end of his speech, Mr Devally strayed a bit. Remember, whether you approve or don't approve of the defendants' action has nothing to do with it. They thought it right. The law says they don't have to be right in their honest belief. None of us is suggesting that the defendants' action is being prosecuted or defended because we are either for or against the war. They are charged with damaging property without lawful excuse. You must be convinced beyond reasonable doubt that they had no lawful excuse. Otherwise you must acquit."

Throughout the three trials, Michael O'Higgins – cool, confident, learned, quick-witted – had been the favourite of the amateur lawyers in the public galleries. An extra buzz went around the room when he stood to give his closing speech.

He began: "In this case there are big questions of life, of evidence, of law...." He then doubled O'Kelly's three principles with six key questions, though in the end his speech wandered over much further ground, mixing law and politics in a rich stew.

Why had the defendants "disabled an American war-plane on the eve of what was anticipated to be and turned out to be a bloody war?... No one phrase can answer this for even one of them. All of them had a primary reason, namely to protect the lives of people who would be the end 'receivers' of this war.... They're not hillbillies or vigilantes, not seeking to ram their views down anyone's throats, not looking for any favours; they simply ask meekly and humbly that the law be applied." The law, he said, allowed damage to protect life and property, when the accused had an honest belief that the action was necessary and it was reasonable in circumstances as they believed them to be.

"Iraq was on its knees: this is not an empty belief. And their belief that the war was illegal was well-supported.... these are not fringe people – their views are supported in the highest echelons."

He recalled the figure of 1.5 million dead through sanctions in Iraq, a number already known in 2003. Three years later, he said, "the events of 2003 have faded. In that year we were in the eighth year of the Celtic Tiger. There was a great fear of going back to the bad times, economically, that we had come through. It became clear in the debate of the time that what the government was doing in letting the U.S. military use Shannon was based on their fear that U.S. companies would get up and go and the economy would regress. The economy was the important factor. If you disagree with this viewpoint, fair enough; but if you agree, you then begin to understand how we can see 1.5 million people die and take no action to prevent it.

"The Germans who stayed silent during the Holocaust were not bad people. The Irish who didn't get angry were not bad people. They were just people who were wrapped up in their own business.

"When you do something… you don't know whether or not the effect will gather the force of a tsunami. History has shown that people who go against the grain make a difference. You can't conclude it won't make a difference. What you can say is that it's reasonable to assume that it might make a difference.

"Rosa Parks got on a bus and set off a chain reaction. Black people were marching all over America. So much so that their feet were sore, but their souls were resting….

"An idea is a very powerful thing. Deirdre Clancy said that what she hoped for was naïve. We need naïve people if we are to have a better future. The fact that they don't realize their hopes doesn't mean that the act was unreasonable."

O'Higgins complimented Devally, but characterized the prosecutor as asking the jury "to decide what the law was. You are here two weeks and he asks you to decide where the line is between what is lawful and what is not. You should not do that. You should pose the questions referable to the act. You should ask: Did they cause damage? What was their purpose? What were the circumstances? And, finally, was their conduct reasonable in those circumstances?…

"Finally, Mr Devally agrees that these are people with great sincerity who have suffered. On any audit they have put far more into this than they can ever get out of it. But they are not professional agitators. They are professional people who have always worked, honorable people who have given of their time for others. They are not seduced by the glossy magazine lifestyle. They are imbued with great courage. When they heard that over 500,000 small children had died because of sanctions they reacted. They said 'No, we are bound to do something about this.'"

He concluded by telling the 12: "It is an enormous privilege for you to have served on this jury."

On the strength of those closing arguments, the defendants and their supporters were hopeful. On the other hand, Dublin juries tend to convict, at a rate of more than 95 per cent. And starting on the Friday morning, July 21st, you could feel the heat of those words draining away during Judge Reynolds's interminable charge to the jury. Its content was fine; its length seemed excessive, especially since it was forcing the jury to stay on the case over the weekend – though perhaps she was mercifully ensuring that they wouldn't be deliberating, and thus potentially sequestered, on a nice weekend in late July.

The judge summarized every piece of evidence the jury had heard. On the key points of law, she concentrated on the importance of the word 'reasonable.' She said that it was immaterial whether the beliefs of the accused were right or wrong, once they were honestly held. However, even if the beliefs were honestly held, the jury must decide whether the actions of the accused were reasonable, she said. While the examples given by both the prosecution and defence were helpful, the facts of this case alone must be considered. An objective test must be applied, where the jury must ask themselves, given the burden of proof on the prosecution, if they were satisfied that the actions were *not* reasonable.

Judge Reynolds said that it would be impossible not to have a strong emotional response to some of the evidence heard during the trial. She was not asking the jury to suspend their humanity, but to look at the facts as dispassionately and analytically as possible.

Inasmuch as she reflected on the defendants' character, it was in terms of seeming approbation: the accused referred to themselves as peace activists, she said, and were "intelligent and educated."

It took until Monday afternoon, July 24th, for her to finish her instructions. The jury were sent out in the late afternoon to reach a verdict. At 6pm, a request came in from the jury for a copy of Section 6 of the Criminal Damage Act 1991 and Section 21 of the Non-Fatal Offences Against the Person Act 1997, which amended it. Judge Reynolds said that it was not usual to give written statutes to the jury. Instead she read out relevant sections from the legislation and said that, if the jury wished, she would explain again how the law should be applied. It was, said one observer, a bit like the Catholic Church, which reserved the right to interpret God's words. The jury were acting like Protestants, wanting to read the words for themselves.

The jury, having not reached a verdict, was sequestered overnight.

On Tuesday morning, the tension was high. On the way into court Ciaron and Damien had a spat: Damien admonished Ciaron for a lack of non-violent discipline, and Ciaron called his young friend a "pious little prick."

In the courtroom Judge Reynolds brought the jury in and reiterated her original direction regarding matters of law. She reminded the jury that matters of fact were their domain, while matters of law were hers. She again set out the defence of lawful excuse in relation to damaging property. It sounded good. But Ciaron O'Reilly's head was buzzing, so he asked a distinctly unlegalistic friend what the judge had been saying. The friend summarized how he had heard the judge's final instruction to the jury: "Well, you can take a hammer to a war-plane, or you can bomb a country killing thousands of innocent people – you decide which is worse." Judge Reynolds had obviously said nothing of the sort, but the vibration of acquittal was somehow in the air.

After three hours and six minutes of deliberation, incorporating an overnight stay at a city-center hotel, the jurors returned verdicts of not-guilty on both charges against all the accused.

In the midst of the excitement, the five put their statement together:

> The jury is the conscience of the community chosen randomly from Irish society. The conscience of the community has spoken. The government has no popular mandate in providing the civilian Shannon airport to service the US war machine in its illegal invasion and occupation of Iraq.
>
> In 1996 in Liverpool the Jury acquittal of the four 'ploughshares' women contributed to the end of arms exports to the Suharto dictatorship in Indonesia and the independence of East Timor.
>
> The decision of this jury should be a message to London, Washington DC and the Dail that Ireland wants no part in waging war on the people of Iraq. Refuelling of US warplanes at Shannon Airport should cease immediately.

The verdict went out on the newswires and was picked up by newspapers and broadcasters around the world. It merited a short report in *Time* magazine. However, for the Irish media, the fact that Dublin had hosted the world's first ever unanimous jury acquittal of Ploughshares defendants didn't seem to merit much attention. There were virtually no front-page stories – except in *Daily Ireland*, the soon-to-be-defunct Belfast-based left-leaning daily – and very few follow-up interviews with the accused.

You had to laugh at the media in the aftermath of the acquittal, if you didn't want to cry. (O'Reilly would get tired of repeating: "Why do we insist on talking about media outlets as though they were there to provide a public service?") The tabloid *Irish Star* alone presented the legal basis for the acquittal clearly and cogently. (Its rival, the *Irish Sun*, was more taken with the "eerie coincidence" that a medieval psalter, supposedly left open, many centuries ago, at a scriptural verse about war, was discovered in a midlands bog on the very day of their acquittal.) Elsewhere, news stories were written by reporters who hadn't followed even the last trial – they had arrived at the Four Courts en masse as word of the acquittal spread – and pundits produced shelf-loads of half-baked conclusions. Typically, these involved ignorance of the specific statutory defence in this case (involving protection of life and/or property, and a requirement of reasonableness in the act) and, thus, unwarranted but dramatic rhetoric about the 'precedent' that had been set.

In the top-selling daily, the *Irish Independent*, daily columnist Ian O'Doherty said the verdict was "baffling" but at least, on a positive note, provided a legal license for "taking a hammer to some hippie's car" since he would be doing it "in good conscience and for the public good." Matt Cooper in the Irish edition of Rupert Murdoch's *Sunday Times* wrote to similar effect: "Based on [the] decision, any defendant charged with a violent act who can argue successfully that the crime was commit-ted to achieve a greater good can feel confident their case will get a decent hearing." Cooper also asserted incorrectly that Judge Mathews had rejected the 'lawful excuse' defence in the pre-trial hearings. In the *Sunday Independent* (Ireland's best-selling newspaper) columnist and right-wing ideological guru Eoghan Harris suggested that the logic of the verdict could have terrible bearing on, say, a murder charge: he could "kill a cop in the course of my anti-American activities and claim that my conscience compelled me to do it." (Harris, some distance removed from the anti-American activities of his Communist youth, had apparently somehow missed the closing speeches about the limits of the statutory defence. Oh well.) Henry McKean on NewsTalk 106 radio ("at the end of the day, they did commit a crime") and Emer O'Kelly in the *Sunday Independent* ("what happened at Shannon airport was a massive crime") both attributed crimes to people who had just been acquitted of those crimes. Luckily for these journalists, the Pitstop Ploughshares were not keen on wasting more years of their lives chasing the media through defamation cases.

If the verdict had happened three years earlier, it would have merited a march straight down to Government Buildings. At this point, however, the reaction from the defendants and their friends was something rather quieter. They spent much of the afternoon of the jury's decision chatting and drinking cups of tea in a Franciscan hall just across the River Liffey from the courthouse. In the evening a few dozen more supporters turned up at a pub for the celebration party – as supporters in Dublin are wont to do – but this too was relatively low-key, an occasion for quiet satisfaction and sad reflection on the previous three-and-a-half years, not for anything like triumphalism. The inevitable 'what next?' questions tended to be personal at least as much as political, and none of the defendants seemed entirely secure in their answers. An air of bewilderment hung over the gatherings. A few of the lawyers looked in on the way to their own celebrations, but for all the affection that had built up over the years it was clear those relationships were now effectively at an end.

The US embassy statement expressing concern at the verdict and seeking a meeting with the government was firmly knocked back by the now-Minister for Foreign Affairs, Dermot Ahern. The courts were independent and it was not for government officials to be discussing their deliberations, he said. Unalloyed joy being a rare Irish commodity, a few voices were raised quietly among the Pitstop Ploughshares supporters, wondering if perhaps the government had even got the verdict it wanted: a nice little Irish slap – rather than a hammering – for Bush and his unpopular warmongering ilk, but no lasting threat to the status quo, at Shannon Airport and beyond.

Epilogue

FTER THE VERDICT CIARON O'REILLY COULDN'T TAKE THE risk that there might be some positive momentum to capitalize upon and that he had failed to do so. The other risk was looking foolish, of course, but that one rarely seemed to faze him. At a press conference the day after the verdict he announced his intention, inspired by Bertrand Russell, to gather 100 people who would take nonviolent direct action at a future date to close down Shannon Airport (temporarily, of course) if the Irish government did not move to demilitarize it. Over the coming weeks there were public meetings all over the country, and Damien Moran got to plug the plea on another *Would You Believe* TV documentary, this time devoted to him, but the numbers committed to action never seemed to move past a couple of dozen or so (myself included), and many of them were only willing to act if the total who were prepared to be arrested at least approached 100. Which it never remotely did.

The main effects of the 'threat', as the Clare-based media insisted on calling it, was to stir up some of the local politicians to their old passions, and to cause the state to spend literally millions of extra euro on security at the airport. The police, complete with helicopter and seemingly countless little hand-held cameras, got at least one big day out in late October at Shannon when they may well have outnumbered the marchers at a rally organized by Anti-War Ireland. This latter was a group including Deirdre Clancy, Fintan Lane and me, something of an alternative to the Irish Anti-War Movement, itself now a shadow of its former glory. The Shannon event was a first return to the airport – or at least to its perimeter – for Ciaron and Deirdre, who led a symbolic coffin to the airport entrance, accompanied by three US veterans of the Iraq war.

The acquittal did have one surprising effect in the North of Ireland. Just two weeks after the verdict, in Derry, three members of the Socialist Workers Party – usually rather critical of the Ploughshares approach – joined with six dissident republicans to damage equipment at the offices of the multinational weapons-technology company Raytheon, long a target for peace-and-justice activists, whose equipment was being used by Israel in the attacks on Lebanon. They were arrested and faced serious charges. Despite the political differences, their supporters were frank about the inspirational effect of the Shannon Five case.

While Ciaron was getting rather downcast about the low uptake for direct action at Shannon – though he was boosted by interest from an American Shakespeare scholar in the thinking behind *MacBush* – Deirdre was putting public and private work into building anti-war activities and structures in Ireland for the long haul. The other three ex-defendants had left the country. Nuin was the subject of occasional 'sightings' at locations across Europe, but was otherwise out of contact. Karen was also quiet in Scotland, coping with personal and political sadness and, she told me, planting hundreds of trees.

Karen wasn't the only one planting. Just as I finished a first draft of this book in early 2007, I coincidentally got a text message on my phone from Damien Moran: "Greetings from rainy Warsaw. Just comin back from demo outside US Embassy org'd by anarchists. I planted 20 roses in 20 permanent flower pots directly outside embassy in commemoration of all victims of US wars. Hopefully their staff will realize the consequences of their work every time they see them & have a change of heart. About 40 of us took part." For some reason this message reduced me to tears.

Deirdre Clancy has said that the most annoying thing about being one of the Shannon Five, before and after the verdict, was the tendency of people to approach her and say, "You make me feel so guilty. I wish I had your commitment." Deirdre's annoyance was because she thought people should concentrate on what they can do themselves to resist war, and not elevate or separate her because she had felt able to employ a particular tactic.

But anyway, as my own dad used to say, guilt is a wasted emotion. Don't feel guilty; don't wish. Do something. Daniel Berrigan, in the foreword to Ciaron O'Reilly's book *Remembering Forgetting*, puts it well: "There's no free trip, there's a toll gate along every highway. Stand somewhere, walk there, sit there, refuse there, sing there, get dragged away there. Pay up, or join the inhumans."

Index

AK Press

Ordering Information

AK Press
674-A 23rd Street
Oakland, CA 94612-1163
U.S.A
(510) 208-1700
www.akpress.org
akpress@akpress.org

AK Press
PO Box 12766
Edinburgh, EH8 9YE
Scotland
(0131) 555-5165
www.akuk.com
ak@akedin.demon.uk

The addresses above would be delighted to provide you with the latest complete AK catalog, featuring several thousand books, pamphlets, zines, audio products, video products, and stylish apparel published & distributed by AK Press. Alternatively, check out our websites for the complete catalog, latest news and updates, events, and secure ordering.

Also Available from AK Press

The first audio collection from Alexander Cockburn on compact disc.

Beating the Devil

Alexander Cockburn, ISBN 13: 9781902593494 • CD • $14.98

In this collection of recent talks, maverick commentator Alexander Cockburn defiles subjects ranging from Colombia to the American presidency to the Missile Defense System. Whether he's skewering the fallacies of the war on drugs or illuminating the dark crevices of secret government, his erudite and extemporaneous style warms the hearts of even the stodgiest cynics of the left.

Available from CounterPunch/AK Press

The Case Against Israel

by Michael Neumann

Wielding a buzzsaw of logic, Professor Neumann dismantles plank-by-plank the Zionist rationale for Israel as religious state entitled to trample upon the basic human rights of non-Jews. Along the way, Neumann also offers a passionate amicus brief for the plight of the Palestinian people.

Other Lands Have Dreams: From Baghdad to Pekin Prison

by Kathy Kelly

At a moment when so many despairing peace activists have thrown in the towel, Kathy Kelly, a witness to some of history's worst crimes, never relinquishes hope. Other Lands Have Dreams is literary testimony of the highest order, vividly recording the secret casualties of our era, from the hundreds of thousands of Iraqi children inhumanely denied basic medical care, clean water and food by the US overlords to young mothers sealed inside the sterile dungeons of American prisons in the name of the merciless war on drugs.

Dime's Worth of Difference: Beyond the Lesser of Two Evils

Edited by Alexander Cockburn and Jeffrey St. Clair

Everything you wanted to know about one-party rule in America.

Whiteout: the CIA, Drugs and the Press

by Alexander Cockburn and Jeffrey St. Clair, Verso.

The involvement of the CIA with drug traffickers is a story that has slouched into the limelight every decade or so since the creation of the Agency. In Whiteout, here at last is the full saga.

Been Brown So Long It Looked Like Green to Me: the Politics of Nature

by Jeffrey St. Clair, Common Courage Press.

Covering everything from toxics to electric power plays, St. Clair draws a savage profile of how money and power determine the state of our environment, gives a vivid account of where the environment stands today and what to do about it.

Imperial Crusades: Iraq, Afghanistan and Yugoslavia

by Alexander Cockburn and Jeffrey St. Clair, Verso.

A chronicle of the lies that are now returning each and every day to haunt the deceivers in Washington and London, the secret agendas and the underreported carnage of these wars. We were right and they were wrong, and this book proves the case. Never leave home without it.

Why We Publish CounterPunch

By Alexander Cockburn and Jeffrey St. Clair

FIFTEEN YEARS AGO WE FELT UNHAPPY ABOUT THE STATE OF RADICAL JOURN-alism. It didn't have much edge. It didn't have many facts. It was politically timid. It was dull. CounterPunch was founded. We wanted it to be the best muckraking newsletter in the country. We wanted it to take aim at the consensus of received wisdom about what can and cannot be reported. We wanted to give our readers a political roadmap they could trust.

A decade later we stand firm on these same beliefs and hopes. We think we've restored honor to muckraking journalism in the tradition of our favorite radical pamphleteers: Edward Abbey, Peter Maurin and Ammon Hennacy, Appeal to Reason, Jacques René Hébert, Tom Paine and John Lilburne.

Every two weeks CounterPunch gives you jaw-dropping exposés on: Congress and lobbyists; the environment; labor; the National Security State.

"CounterPunch kicks through the floorboards of lies and gets to the founda-tion of what is really going on in this country", says Michael Ratner, attorney at the Center for Constitutional Rights. "At our house, we fight over who gets to read CounterPunch first. Each issue is like spring after a cold, dark winter."

The Secret Language of the Crossroads

How the Irish Invented Slang

By Daniel Cassidy

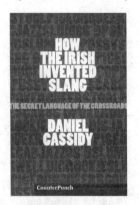

In *How the Irish Invented Slang: The Secret Language of the Crossroad*, Daniel Cassidy co-director and founder of the Irish Studies Program at New College of California cuts through two hundred years worth of Anglo academic "baloney" and reveals the massive, hidden influence of the Irish language on the American language.

Irish words and phrases are scattered all across the American language, regional and class dialects, colloquialism, slang, and specialized jargons like gambling, in the same way Irish-Americans have been scattered across the crossroads of North America for five hundred years.

In a series of essays, including: "Decoding the Gangs of New York," "How the Irish Invented Poker and American Gambling Slang," "The Sanas (Etymology) of Jazz," "Boliver of Brooklyn," and in a *First Dictionary of Irish-American Vernacular*, Cassidy provides the hidden histories and etymologies of hundreds of so-called slang words that have defined the American language and culture like *dude, sucker, swell, poker, faro, cop, scab, fink, moolah, fluke, knack, ballyhoo, baloney,* as well as the hottest word of the 20th century, *jazz*.